IT'S ALL ABOUT

The Dress

IT'S ALL ABOUT

The Dress

*Savvy Secrets, Priceless Advice, and Inspiring Stories
to Help You Find "the One"*

RANDY FENOLI

Photographs by

François Dischinger

GRAND CENTRAL
Life & Style
NEW YORK · BOSTON

On page 2, the childhood photos of Randy Fenoli are from the Fenoli family collection.
On page 6, the Dessy catalog cover photo is copyright © Jacques Malignon, originally published in *Modern Bride*, a Condé Nast publication.
All other photographs are copyright © 2011 by François Dischinger.
Used by permission.

Grand Central Life & Style
Hachette Book Group
237 Park Avenue, New York, NY 10017

www.HachetteBookGroup.com

Grand Central Life & Style is an imprint of Grand Central Publishing.
The Grand Central Life & Style name and logo are trademarks of Hachette Book Group, Inc.

The publisher is not responsible for websites (or their content) that are not owned by the publisher.

Printed in the United States of America

First Edition: November 2011

10 9 8 7 6 5 4 3 2 1

Library of Congress Control Number: 2011927083
ISBN 978-0-446-58507-1

Designed by Hoffman Creative

Dedicated to

My mother, who told me when I was a child I could achieve anything. She continues to give me strength, love, courage, advice, and support.

My sister, Linda: You always made me feel loved.

My wonderful partner, Michael. I love you. Thanks for putting up with me and my crazy life.

My dogs Maggie and Bandit, who make me smile every time I walk through the door.

And to brides and women everywhere… I hope you realize how truly beautiful you are!

Hello, Beautiful!

I can't tell you the number of times women say to me, "Randy, why can't I take you shopping with me? I wish there was a little Randy that I could slip into my pocket or drop into my handbag!" Although I wish I could hop right into that Birkin, I simply can't be there in person for all of you. So I decided to create this book and give you the next best thing.

After almost twenty years designing and helping brides choose dresses, I know bridal wear literally from the inside out. And I know that selecting the perfect gown for your dream day may feel a little overwhelming. There's one thing I can promise you: *Your* dress is out there, waiting for you. And I'm going to help you find it.

Shopping for your wedding gown shouldn't be a chore. It should be fun!

There are three key things I will do for you:

EDUCATE *you about wedding gowns*
ELEVATE *your self-confidence throughout the process of finding a dress*
EMPOWER *you to be the best and most beautiful bride you can be*

When I talk about finding the right gown, I'm not talking about just any gown that *I* or your bridal consultant or your best friend thinks is right for you. I'm talking about the gown that you fall in love with. The gown that makes you cry, and makes you glow! It's the dress that tells the story of you and your fiancé. It's the dress that will make you throw your shoulders back when you look in the mirror and say:

This is *it*.

From the moment you try it on to the moment you walk down that aisle, one dress will transform you into an extraordinary bride just like it did for the other brides on the pages of this book.

Like the title says, it's all about the dress.

Your dress.

Love,

Contents

MY STORY

*Believe it or not, my love for fashion
began on a farm*

When I was a kid, I'd get up at 5 AM to take care of our cows. Yes, cows. We lived on a farm in southern Illinois with 163 acres and a hundred head of cattle.

Today I still get up at 5 AM. But now I do it because I need enough time to choose the right suit, pocket square, necktie, socks, and coordinating cuff links for my day at work. I can't really talk to brides all day about style if I'm not dressed my very best, too! I say, "If you're going to sell luxury, you'd better look luxury!"

My mom grew up during the Great Depression and worked her way up to the rank of second lieutenant army nurse. She ran our household like an army barracks. Dad was a lieutenant colonel in the air force: a career military man with a fierce, fiery temper. There were seven kids in my family: my older sister, my five older brothers, and me. Although I was the smallest of the six boys, I was still expected to carry my weight and be just as tough as my brothers were. I lugged sledgehammers that weighed more than I did! In the winter, we'd break up the ice on one of our seven ponds so the cows could drink.

I tried to fit in even though my father

would make fun of me. He teased me mercilessly because I was so skinny. I remember his bellow: "Randy has to run around inside the shower just to get wet! One day some gust of wind is going to blow him away!"

Truth was: I would have given anything for a gust of wind to blow me off that farm. In my fantasy, it would have been the tornado from *The Wizard of Oz*. Only for me, there was no place but *away from* home! Deep down I knew I didn't fit into this life.

My older sister, Linda, knew it, too. She watched over me like no one else—and brought joy into my daily life. She would get a kick out of dressing me up in her clothes! There's a photo of me at the age of two, standing on the diving board of our backyard pond. I'm dressed up in my sister's one-piece bathing suit, my chest is stuffed with socks, and I have a swim cap on my head!

With seven kids to dress, Mom bought every-thing in bulk and one size up so it would last lon-ger. Sure, I got new outfits, but a lot of the clothes I wore were hand-me-downs. (To this day, I get a little anxious when I walk into a vintage shop.) No matter where I got my clothes, however, I took great care of them. By the time I was five, I was already a master at doing laundry. Seriously! I was great at ironing, too. Even my dad would ask me to iron *his* clothes. (To this day, I iron everything I wear.) I grew so meticulous about my clothes that I defi-nitely washed them too much.

When I was in grade school, Mom bought me a bright red wool jacket with a crest on it. It was perfect for my school photo, and I wore it proudly. After the photo had been taken, I came home and took it off. It needed to be washed, of course, so I headed downstairs to our laundry room. I can still recall feeling the chill of the linoleum floor and the cold metal washing machine as I watched the jacket spin through each cycle. When it was

Top left: When I was two, my sister dressed me up in a one-piece swimsuit.

Top right: My grade school photo in my favorite red wool jacket.

washed, I pulled it out—only to discover that it had shrunk by at least three sizes! I tugged and pulled on the wet wool, but to no avail. The jacket was ruined.

I just knew Mom would be angry with me. But she wasn't. I remember her holding me at arm's length as she said, "I am very proud of you, Randy. You cared. And you tried your best. That's all I can ask."

I couldn't believe it. What a major lesson in love and support! Mom may not have understood everything about me, but in that moment she seemed to acknowledge how important that red jacket was to me. She seemed to understand that clothes mattered to me more than the average kid—or even the average grown-up. Of course, the red jacket incident was also a good lesson in something else: fabric science. Like wool shrinks in water, people!

Watching my sister and mother get dressed up had a huge impact on me. I often rifled through my sister's closet and marveled at her assortment of clothes: 1960s sundresses and 1970s bell-bottoms. But there was one dress in particular—an enormous, strapless, fluffy prom dress with layer upon layer of yellow ruffled tulle—that simply fascinated me. I loved that dress! I wondered: How does someone even *make* a dress like that?

My mother's closet was an even bigger playground. Mom had rows and rows of exotic, beautifully made garments and a vast collection of belts to cinch her tiny waist. Because my parents had been in the military, they'd spent much of their time traveling. Along the way, Mom collected clothes from all over the world. Oh, how I loved the kimonos, robes, and obis from Japan and the Philippines! But the article of clothing I loved the most was a simple dress Mom had purchased

years before, in California: a strapless, daffodil-yellow, cotton organdy dress with little raised white dots and a full circle skirt. It was a 1950s masterpiece. I couldn't understand why she never wore it. I said, "Mom, you would look so beautiful in this dress. Why don't you put it on?" But she always chuckled at me. With seven children and a farm to keep, when would she ever have the time or the occasion to wear yellow dotted organdy?

One hot summer, my brothers and I were working out in the fields, baling hay. As the smallest in the group, I was assigned "water boy" duty. This meant many long trips in the scorching sun carrying jugs of ice water from the house to the guys in the fields.

Then, across the field, Mom appeared—in the dress.

The hem of the organdy skirt caught the breeze, and the fabric seemed to float and billow all around her hips. To me, Mom looked like a movie star. She came right over to where I stood, leaned in, and whispered, "Randy, I wore this dress just for you. Thank you for helping me feel beautiful again."

I wanted to cry. Somehow, this skinny southern Illinois farm boy had managed to show my mom that she could look and feel beautiful even on one of the hottest days in the middle of a field. Somehow, I'd shown how a single dress brought out the true beauty—inside and out—that my mother had been hiding for so many years.

When I was nine years old, Mom purchased a sewing machine. She worked so hard as a nurse and did everything she could to save pennies for our large family. She figured the sewing machine would help her to save even more money. Mom was going to sew curtains and make clothes for us children.

Watching my sister and mother get dressed up in their clothes had a huge impact on me.
I often rifled through my sister's closet and marveled at her assortment of clothes.

One day, she came home with a bolt of blue-and-white cotton faille fabric and tried to make a dress. She quickly discovered that she was all thumbs. She literally could not sew a hem on a terry-cloth towel! Frustrated, she set everything aside: the good scissors, the thread, and of course her good bolt of fabric. Before she left for work one morning, Mom warned me: "Don't touch any of my sewing, Randy!"

Of course, as soon as she was gone, I touched *everything*.

From the numerous dress patterns on Mom's sewing table, I remember plucking out a McCall's pattern with Marlo Thomas posing on the front. (I had a huge crush on Marlo, aka *That Girl*, back then.) By midmorning, I'd laid out all the fabric and pinned down the pattern on our dining room table. Our table was extra-long to accommodate our large family of nine, and it made the perfect pattern table. I cut the fabric and started sewing and in no time I had a dress! Carefully, I ironed the dress and hung it on a hanger. Then I cleaned up the work space so it was spotless.

When Mom came home that night, she saw the dress—the dress I had made—hanging in the door frame.

"Where did this come from?" she asked.

"I made it for you," I said.

Mom was in total shock! She quickly removed the dress from the hanger and tried it on. It was a perfect fit. In fact, she wore that dress to work the very next day.

The following night, Mom returned home with *another* pattern and asked me to make her a skirt.

And of course, I did.

Sewing clothes became an escape for me. It took me away from the farm and distanced me from my father's temper. It brought me even closer to my mother and sister. I was inspired by both of them to appreciate and celebrate a woman's beauty. After high school, I became a professional hairstylist and makeup artist in addition to sewing dresses and making theatrical costumes. I worked hard and saved up enough money to take my life in a new direction.

I moved to New York City and enrolled at the Fashion Institute of Technology (FIT).

FIT was the perfect fit for me. My professors were pleased with my work, even though I stubbornly insisted on designing one type of clothing: evening gowns. Once, I was given an assignment to design five swimsuits. Instead I designed *fifteen gowns* that transformed into swimsuits! It wasn't until the school had a competition to design bridal wear that I knew I'd found my true love in clothing design.

We were asked to sketch and design three different elements: a mood board (a collage of photos and items used for inspiration), a bridal gown, and a bridesmaid's dress.

I decided to create *five* sets of each. When the judges selected their top ten, five of the ten designs they chose were mine. Then they chose *one* design for me to actually create. I worked hard, draping fabric, cutting patterns, and hand finishing the details of the dress. Because I was so thin, I was a sample size and used *myself* as my own fit model. For this reason, I consider myself lucky. I'm able to understand dresses from concept to creation *and* even know what they feel like *on*!

Before the winners of the contest were announced, I got a surprising phone call on the pay phone at the dormitory. Vivian Dessy Diamond, who was one of the judges of the contest, and her husband, Paul Diamond—two big names in the bridal industry—asked me to design for them. I was in shock! No FIT student had ever landed his or her own label *before* graduation. Of course, I said yes.

I did end up winning that contest. However, the real prize for me was having my name on two labels: Randy Fenoli for Dessy Creations and Randy Fenoli for the Diamond Collection. My designs went down the runway four months after I got my diploma. What a graduation gift!

Everything came fast and furious after that. Randy Fenoli wedding gowns were featured on the pages and covers of all the major bridal magazines. In both 1999 and 2000, I was honored with the Design Excellence in the Bridal Industry (DEBI) award. For nearly ten years, I designed and created two collections annually and traveled to almost twenty-five trunk shows per year. This meant meeting with thousands of brides across the country to promote my latest collections. One

Top left:
My original sketch of the dress that won the bridal contest at FIT.

Bottom left:
The first wedding dress I ever designed: a halter, which was radical for the time.

of those trunk shows was at Kleinfeld in Brooklyn, New York. A record-breaking ninety-three dresses were sold in a single week.

After the tragedy of September 11, I decided to move to New Orleans to open my own dress shop. I would design custom, made-to-order bridal, debutante, and Mardi Gras gowns. Two weeks before I was supposed to open my shop, however, my plans were disrupted by one angry lady: Hurricane Katrina.

I consider myself blessed that I didn't lose my home. However, all of my supplies to open my store were in a storage unit that was washed away in the storm. I ultimately decided to leave New Orleans and head back to a place I knew well, my old "home," New York City. I was armed with nothing more than a strong desire to get back to what I loved best: bridal.

Several salons offered me jobs in New York, but I landed back at the place I'd been so successful before: Kleinfeld. They created a unique position for me with the title of "fashion director." And so I became stylist and adviser to more than fifteen thousand brides each year. I was also asked to appear in a TV show they were filming at the salon for TLC called *Say Yes to the Dress*. Maybe you've seen it?

During these years, I've met literally thousands of brides on all sides of the business. Along the way, I have designed and produced bridal gowns, and stood there with many brides as they tried to figure out which dress fit them best and made them feel beautiful.

I believe *all* women are beautiful! They just need reassurance and guidance in choosing the right dress that will enhance their natural beauty. For me, a piece of clothing is much more than just a piece of fabric. It can make you *feel*.

I remember watching a show once in which Oprah Winfrey brought Christmas to children in Africa. As presents, she gave all the boys soccer balls, and all the girls received baby dolls. And all the children got new uniforms for school.

To everyone's surprise, the gift the children liked most was the clothes! They said that when they put their uniform on, they no longer felt poor.

The truth is, wearing clothes you love can make *anyone* stand taller, smile wider, and feel richer. Clothes can tell the world where you've been, where you're going, who you are, and who you want to be. Clothes can tell people your story.

Every bride and groom has a unique story of how their relationship began and who they are as a couple. Your wedding and your wedding gown can help tell that story to your guests. From the moment your guests see you and watch you walk down that aisle, your wedding dress affirms your strength, beauty, confidence, and *story* in every way.

What may be most informative and inspirational are the many bride-and-groom stories I've included and will share with you. Each one of my brides had a reason she connected with and purchased her wedding gown. I hope you will see a little piece of yourself while reading their stories.

There is so much information about weddings and how to choose the perfect dress; it's easy for a bride to get overwhelmed. I don't want you to get overwhelmed by too much information. This is why I've written my book with chapters that are simple and help answer a bride's main questions and concerns. In this book, I will give you only my best suggestions and advice.

To begin, I've come up with what I call the *five essentials* you will need to help you find your perfect wedding gown. Each one is outlined in its own chapter:

1. Your Story
2. Your Plan
3. Your Gown
4. Your Body
5. Your Look

Once you understand these five essentials, you'll be ready for your appointment—and ready to say yes to your dress. Along the way, I will also give you my "Randy Rules." For every rule throughout this process, remember: There will always be an exception. In fact, that is my first Randy Rule.

As much as I like bending rules, however, I do realize that having some straightforward

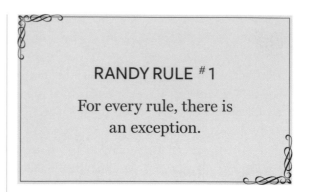

RANDY RULE #1

For every rule, there is an exception.

guidelines *can* be very helpful when selecting your dress and making important decisions about your wedding. I will also guide you through your alterations and give you my advice for dressing your bridesmaids, mothers, and the men for your wedding.

In the end, when you finally do say "I do" to the man of your dreams, you'll be wearing the dress of your dreams.

All the models in my book are real brides; they vary in age, shape, and ethnicity. All are beautiful!

CHAPTER ONE

YOUR STORY

This is not your mother's wedding book

Whenever I hear a couple tell their personal story, I connect with them on a completely different level. These stories often touch me deeply and sometimes even bring me to tears. I love hearing how two people met and how they fell in love. I admire them for the challenges and obstacles they have overcome to get where they are today. I've honestly met hundreds of thousands of brides over the years. Often I think I've seen and heard it all. But one thing I've learned is that no matter how many stories brides tell me, one thing remains the same for all couples. Each has a unique, intimate, and personal story to tell. We create our lives each day by the choices we make. I like to think that we're adding new chapters to the story of our lives all the time. I am passionate about owning my story. I want you to be passionate about owning yours.

When you are pronounced husband and wife you will turn around, and face your guests, and realize you have just created a new family unit! In this moment, everything about the couple says to their guests: This is who we are! Your attire will say: This is our taste level in clothing. The food you serve at your reception says: This is the food we would serve you if you were guests in our home. The music at your reception says: This is the music we like to dance and party to. Everything about your wedding says: *This is us. This is our story. This is our brand.* And to begin that story, what will everyone be looking at? . . . You and your dress.

For many years, women purchased wedding dresses based on preconceived notions about what they were "supposed" to wear or what they were told they "should" wear. Wedding details were carefully prescribed by others. Brides worked from manufactured checklists. We got help from mothers, aunts, and friends who had already been through the process.

And we still do. But today's weddings have become much more about a couple's self-expression. Today couples may still want to honor traditions, but they also want their wedding to be unique and to feature the unexpected.

I remember hearing an incredible story of a bride who had a difficult struggle with breast cancer. This courageous woman had lost all of her hair during her chemotherapy treatments, but she didn't let that get in the way of her wedding. She was simply grateful to be alive. And her story of survival was so powerful that everyone at her wedding was moved to honor it. On the day of the ceremony, in admiration of her courage, the groomsmen revealed that they had all shaved their heads; the bridesmaids walked down the aisle wearing wigs just like the bride wore.

Everything about that deeply personal moment celebrated the bride's story.

Your wedding day should be similar. I'm not saying that your groomsmen need to shave their heads; however, your guests will want to better understand your story as a couple and to be a part of it. The more personal and the more unique you make your wedding story, the more your guests will enjoy it. Your story is distinctive, and unlike any other couple's story that has come before it.

In this book, I've included dozens of stories from brides I've met. The stories are dramatic, romantic, nostalgic, heroic, and fantastic! But the thing that makes me most proud is that all of these stories are *true*. And all of the brides are real just like you. No models were hired for my book or appear on these pages. These brides are real women in their twenties, thirties, forties, fifties, and even sixties. They're tall, petite, slim, curvaceous—even tattooed. And their stories are real!

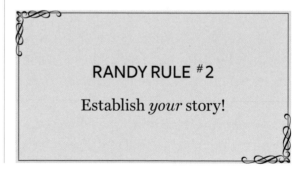

RANDY RULE #2

Establish *your* story!

Each one of these brides was true to her story. Clockwise from left: Kate, Jessica, and Jessica.

How to Tell Your Story

A story takes time to develop. Your story as a couple began when you first met. For just a moment, let's imagine your wedding story. Let's step away from the pile of bridal books (other than this one, of course) that you have stacked on your coffee table. Put away the bridal gown pictures you've been tearing out of magazines. Stop surfing the Internet for the latest wedding trends—at least for a little while. I promise we'll get back to all those things later.

For now, let's look closely at the story of your life since you met your fiancé. Start with the moment you first saw each other.

Do you remember the way your fiancé gazed into your eyes? Was there a moment when you just "knew" he would be the one you married? How did your fiancé propose to you? Was it in front of a large crowd or was it just the two of you? Maybe the proposal took place in a grand setting like the top of the Empire State Building—or maybe it was someplace intimate and special to the two of you. Or maybe *you* proposed to him! Did he give you a new diamond or his great-grandmother's hundred-year-old ring? What kind of a bride have you always dreamed of being? What kind of bride do you want to be?

Ask yourself a wide range of questions to figure out the specific details of your story. Take notes on paper if you want. Sometimes the smallest detail can be the one that is most revealing and tells the greatest story. Almost every day an anxious bride will come to me and say, "Look, Randy, I don't really have a story. My story is I'm getting married and I need a dress. I came to you because you're the expert. You're supposed to be able to take one look at me and then go pick out the right dress." I honestly want to say, "Sure! Now let me go and get my magic wand…"

> Ask yourself a wide range of questions to figure out the specific details of your story.

I know what's really happening here. I'm working with a bride who hasn't given a lot of thought to her story and is not clear about how she wants to look on her wedding day.

I usually tell my bride to first take a deep breath. Then I ask her to tell me how she wants to look on her wedding day. Sometimes when I ask brides this question, they simply give me a blank stare. And let's be honest, who wouldn't get a little

QUESTIONS TO HELP YOU DEFINE YOUR STORY

- What was your first or your most memorable date?

- What things do you like doing together?

- What are your aspirations and goals?

- What is your personal style?

- What is your fiancé's style?

- Where do you like to shop?

- What are your favorite hobbies?

- What kind of music do you listen to?

- What kind of foods do you like to eat?

- What colors and textures do you like best?

- When you go out, what do you like to wear?

- What Is your favorite way to spend an evening together?

- What is your favorite place to vacation?

- What specific words best describe you?

- Your fiancé?

- What words best describe you as a couple?

anxious thinking about all the details involved in planning a wedding?

Then I ask the bride: How do you want your dress to make you *feel* and what do you want it to say to your guests? Do you want to look sexy, understated, modern, chic, traditional? Or maybe you want your dress to have a vintage feeling?

Slowly but surely, my brides begin to talk. In a matter of moments, they become relaxed and the words begin to flow.

With a few key words about her and her fiancé,

maybe the type of silhouette she would like to wear, and maybe the amount she would like to spend, we begin to form a clear picture of the bride's story. Armed with this information, I'm usually able to select a dress especially for that bride.

And as soon as you find *your* story, you'll be one step closer to finding *your* perfect dress, too. Because so much about your bridal gown selection hinges on your story, I strongly recommend that you refine the details of your story *before* you head into a salon. I want you to have your

At age sixty-two, Linda was fortunate enough to find the man of her dreams.

Finding a gown is like finding a husband.
Sometimes you fall in love with the first guy you meet;
sometimes it's the hundred-and-first guy.

story mapped out in your head or even on paper *before* you start shopping. If you don't have a clear picture and your story figured out, you will probably find this process a lot more challenging. Now, I don't expect you to be able to envision the exact dress you will wear or know all of its specific details; however, even the smallest details and key words can give your consultant great insight. Remember the answers to the questions you just gave on page 15. Share them with your consultant.

I've seen so many brides get overwhelmed by their first wedding gown consultation. They don't know what to do or who to listen to. Often they bring in a huge entourage that is vocal about their opinions on the dresses. Meanwhile, there's my bride, standing on the pedestal in the middle of the showroom—and she's completely silent! And although she may well be a successful career woman, right now she can't even find her voice or a few choice words to explain to me what *she* likes. Some of my most outspoken brides are often at a loss for words while gown shopping.

The fact is that any bride—even the most organized, even *you*—may get overwhelmed by the process of finding a wedding gown.

Maybe it's because you never realized how much thought goes into buying an important dress. Maybe it's because you don't have the language or vocabulary necessary to communicate what you want and need in a dress. Face it, you're not Elizabeth Taylor. You haven't done this eight times before.

On the other hand, I have brides who come into the salon with an incredible story, claiming to know *exactly* what they want. They confidently produce a pile of pictures of dresses from magazines or downloaded from the Internet. However, as soon as the consultant and I begin to pull these dresses, things get complicated.

Sometimes the gowns she's chosen simply don't work. What happens *then*?

Even if you are sure you know what dresses you want, you may not find the one you love right away. I tell my brides not to worry; there are no problems here, only challenges. You may need to open your mind to alternative suggestions and try on something else that a consultant recommends. I say finding a gown is like finding a husband. Sometimes you fall in love with the first guy you meet; sometimes it's the hundred-and-first guy. Is your fiancé tall, dark, and handsome like you dreamed he'd be? Maybe he's turned out to be short, blond, and blue-eyed. What then?

You never know what you might discover or fall in love with when you shop for a dress. It may be something you never thought of trying on! You may need a little extra encouragement from your consultant. You may need help *translating* your story into a wedding gown.

I am here to educate, elevate, and empower you to find your story even when roadblocks turn up. I'm here to help you find your way—even when you feel like you're lost. Most brides I work with have complex stories that combine *many* different aspects of who they are. They sometimes have many different elements to their story they would like to combine into one dress.

What do you do if family tradition requires that you wear Grandma's veil that has been passed down for generations...but you also want to wear a modern-style dress? Can you do *both*? What if you are fuller-figured and you want a very fitted gown that shows off, flatters, and celebrates your curves? Can you find a sexy dress—in a plus size? What if you're in your forties getting married in the Grand Canyon and *you* want to tell your story wearing a poofy, sparkling ball gown, but every magazine article says that at your age you need to find a more understated, more age-appropriate dress?

Ladies, listen closely so you don't miss this:

You must follow your story *wherever* it takes you! That means wear your grandmother's veil with that modern gown. Show off your curves. If you're in your forties and you want a poofy princess ball gown, then by all means, you can—and should—go for it!

Remember this, too: It doesn't matter how long it takes you to find your story. It doesn't matter what other people think about your story. What matters is that you find it, own it, and tell it.

It doesn't matter how long it takes you to find your story.
It doesn't matter what other people think about your story.
What matters is that you find it, own it, and tell it.

Randy's Recap

THE FIRST THING YOU NEED TO DO IS
FIGURE OUT THE "STORY" OF YOU AND YOUR FIANCÉ

•

TO FIND YOUR STORY, DIG DEEP AND ASK YOURSELF
THE RIGHT QUESTIONS

•

KNOW YOUR STORY BEFORE YOU BEGIN
SHOPPING FOR A DRESS

•

ONCE YOU FIND YOUR STORY, YOU WILL FIND YOUR DRESS

•

KEEP AN OPEN MIND WHEN TRYING ON DRESSES:
SOMETIMES THE ONE YOU END UP WITH WILL BE NOTHING
LIKE THE ONE YOU IMAGINED

•

TRY NOT TO GET OVERWHELMED SHOPPING
FOR A WEDDING GOWN

THIS SHOULD BE FUN!

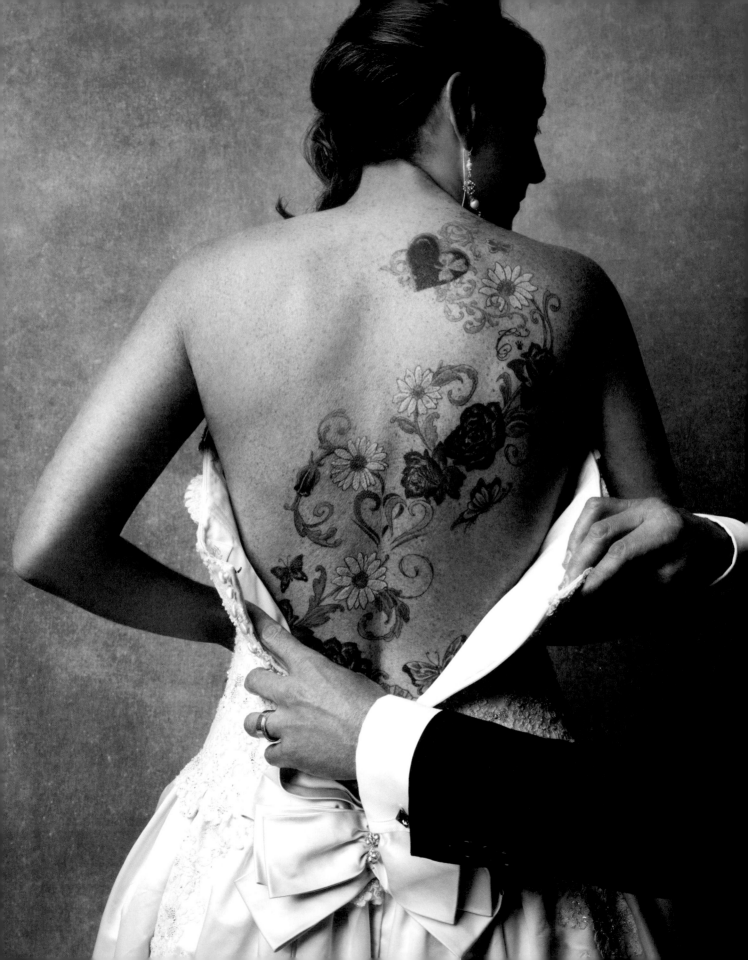

PAM AND SEAN'S $\mathscr{S}$TORY

Hometown	Orillia, Canada (North of Toronto)
Wedding Date	July 29
Location	South Rim of the Grand Canyon, Arizona
Wedding Guests	11
Dress Designer	Eve of Milady

Before they got engaged, Sean and Pam planned a trip to Arizona to visit the Grand Canyon. Before they made the trip, they decided to get tattoos together to celebrate their love for each other. Sean brought Pam's engagement ring with him on the trip and proposed to her after they got their tattoos. The next day while visiting the Grand Canyon, they decided it would be the perfect place to exchange their vows.

When Pam started shopping for the dress of her dreams, the gown that would complement *their* story, the search wasn't easy. Pam rebuffed the idea of an "age-appropriate" gown. And she didn't want something practical. She wanted to look like a princess. "I'd decided to marry at one of the most spectacular settings in the world and I wanted a dress to match," Pam said. "I wasn't a meek bride. I wanted a gown that would be as grand as my destination."

Pam remembers the moment she found her dress: "I swear time stood still as the consultant hung the dress up and fluffed it. I blurted, 'Oh my God! Wait, no!' and stepped back. The dress was everything I wanted. But I was afraid it was going to be too costly. Then my consultant told me that the dress was within my budget. That dress was off the hanger in no time. I put it on, stuck out my chest, and stood up as straight as I could. I *felt* like Wonder Woman. I *looked* like a princess!

"When I met Randy, he understood that although I was a police officer, I needed the ball gown and the grand setting for my wedding." Sean was a nervous wreck the morning of the wedding, but the moment he saw Pam in the dress, his nerves disappeared. The bride's "aisle" was actually a path in the Grand Canyon up to a place called Grandeur Point. As Pam stepped near the edge of the canyon, she remembers the look on Sean's face. He said, "You're the most beautiful bride I've ever seen."

To remember this moment, Pam tattooed her entire wedding bouquet of orange roses, red roses, and daisies down her back! Now, *that's* commitment.

On her honeymoon, Pam had her bridal bouquet tattooed down her back.

CHAPTER TWO

YOUR *P*LAN

A wedding dress is worn once, but photographed forever

I know how you're feeling right now, on the brink of your great big bridal adventure, mind filled with all the romance and excitement of your story. But we're not ready to shop for the dress just yet.

Now that you've figured out your story, you must decide a few practical and essential things before you can move on to your wedding dress purchase. You need to for-mulate a plan that works *with* your story. You need to: establish a budget; decide on the season and time of day; choose a location.

In this chapter, I've broken down the basics for you—including a detailed time-line that will help you to organize the best plan. Just don't forget that this plan needs to connect back to your story.

Establish Your Budget

Now, I'm a big romantic, just like you are. And I can think of nothing *less* romantic than discussing expenses. But the moment you decide to marry, you must talk price and decide upon a budget! Some of the first words out of your consultant's mouth may well be: "How much would you like to spend?"

If you get the budget nailed down early, other decisions will be easier. You won't reach for a gown that costs more than you want to spend—and get your hopes crushed when you see the price tag. You won't try on something that looks perfect—only to find out that it's double your budget. I don't want you to get swept away during the process and find yourself frustrated. By establishing a budget, this can be avoided.

Once I had a bride who brought in a picture of a dress she loved. It was clear to me that she'd been carrying around this photograph for some time. This was the one dress she wanted, and she had her heart set on it. She told the consultant her budget was "up in the air" and tried on the dress—even though the consultant was concerned it might be out of the bride's price range. The dress looked fantastic on her and she was beaming. Sure enough, when the price of the gown was revealed, she was devastated! The dress was well above the limit she wanted to spend. I hoped she might try on other dresses within her price range, but she insisted on wearing that one dress for the entire appointment. Unfortunately, she ended up leaving the salon without a dress. This unhappy situation could have been avoided if she had firmly established her budget.

You can see how important it is to set your budget and be honest about it with yourself *and* your consultant. You can translate your wedding story into the right dress when you know how much money you want to spend. By establishing a budget from the beginning, you can spend more time enjoying the process of planning your wedding and shopping for your gown—from the first appointment all the way to the honeymoon.

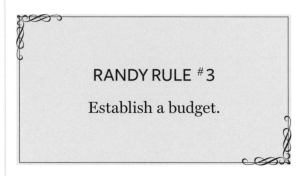

RANDY RULE #3

Establish a budget.

I read the same magazines you do. Sometimes I think the information about how much a wedding gown costs can be a little confusing. Often prices aren't listed for gowns, or they may even be listed incorrectly.

How much should you budget for your gown? Boy, is this a loaded question! And it's a question only you can answer. According to a survey by the Association of Bridal Consultants, brides on average, spend about 6.1 percent of their entire wedding budget on their dress. For me, that seems like a small amount. I believe your wedding gown is probably the most important garment you will ever wear.

Far more important than how much you spend on your dress is that you love it and feel beautiful in it. If you love your gown and feel beautiful, you are going to wear the gown differently. You will

RANDY'S TOP BUDGET QUESTIONS

- How much do I have budgeted for the wedding?

- How much am I willing to spend on the dress?

- Am I paying for the dress?

- Is someone else paying for the dress, and will I need to consider that person's opinion when making the purchase?

- What kind of accessories am I planning to wear—headpiece, veil, jewelry, shoes, et cetera—and have I included them in my budget?

- Have I included alterations in the budget?

- What happens if I fall in love with a dress that is more than I planned on spending?

- Will I be willing to change something else in my wedding budget in order to afford a more expensive dress?

NOTE: If you are a bride with a fuller figure or have a larger bust size, you may incur additional charges when ordering your gown to accommodate your curvaceous figure. More on this in the appointment chapter (page 125).

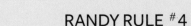

RANDY RULE #4

How you wear your dress
is more important than
how much you spend on it.

stand up taller, you'll smile wider, and your entire body language will be different. For me, confidence is what makes a bride truly beautiful.

Keep in mind that *any* gown you purchase, no matter at what price point, will need some alterations! Even the most moderate price points will require at the very least a hem and a bustle. Now, I know there are brides out there reading this book and cringing at the expensive price tags of some

HOW MUCH DOES A GOWN ACTUALLY COST AND WHAT DO I GET FOR THAT?

The average cost of a wedding gown in America is around $800 to $1,000. Here's my basic guide to what you get for your money:

$500–$1,000

Today there are more choices at this price point, and gowns can be more fashion-forward than in the past. This dress may be purchased from a chain bridal retailer, and it will probably be mass-produced overseas. It will most likely be made from a synthetic material. It may have embroidery and beading, but less fine hand beading and detailing. You will almost certainly not be able to make any changes, like opening up a bra cup or raising a neckline, when ordering your gown. These gowns are usually heavier than gowns made of silk. You may also find a gown at this price at a sample sale. For more about sample sales, see page 30.

$1,000–$2,000

You can find some nice designs and some fashion-forward styles at this price range. Gowns will generally be made of synthetic fabrics. They can have lots of beading and appliqués, although this will not be the fine beading or detailing you will find on more expensive dresses. You will probably not be able to make any changes to these gowns, either.

$2,000–$5,000

This is the most popular opening price point for designer labels, and you should be able to find a nice selection in silk. As the price goes up, so does the quality of fabric, attention to detail, and quality of the beading. This gown will probably be custom-made when ordered, as opposed to being mass-produced. It should be very well made, and can include some fine hand detailing. You'll most likely purchase this dress in a full-service salon where they'll measure you, help you decide on accessories, and order your dress from the designer in your size. Most designers in this price range will allow for custom changes that are usually not available on less expensive dresses, but there will be charges associated with these changes. Note: If you are fuller-busted and need to have a neckline raised or bra cup opened up, you will probably have to purchase a gown in this price point to accommodate your bust.

$5,000–$10,000

At this price, you should be able to find a gown from a well-known wedding dress designer that will be made when you place your order. These dresses will use finer fabrics made of silk, real French lace, and better-quality crystals and beading. The embroidery and beading will most likely come from India or the United States; they're much finer and mostly done by hand. Most designers in this price range will make changes, like adding a sleeve, changing a neckline, or sometimes even changing the fabric. They will also raise a neckline or open a bra cup if you have to accommodate a fuller bust size.

$10,000 +

You can get a gown made to order from a well-known designer, or even a one-of-a-kind custom-made gown. These dresses should only use the finest fabrics, embroidery, crystals, lace, and finishes. The designer will most likely make almost any custom changes that you ask for, sometimes even altering the original design. However, be prepared to pay extra for this.

dresses. And yes, I know what some of you might say: I can get a dress for much less money. This is true. I advise you to find a dress that meets all of your criteria within your budget, or think about ways to rearrange your budget so you can buy the gown that you truly love.

Can you reevaluate how and where you're spending money? What happens when you love a dress that's *over* your budget? You need to be prepared just in case the amount you wanted to spend goes out the window when you see "the dress."

> You need to be prepared
> just in case the amount you want
> to spend goes out the window
> when you see "the dress."

Look, I am a firm believer in budgets. Once you make a wedding budget, lock it in. But I also think that within a set budget, it's important to know you can move money around. You can *find* more money for a higher-priced dress. You just need to get creative.

For example, what if you *borrowed* money from one part of your wedding budget and applied it to another part—namely, your dress? Keep in mind that most brides use around ten to fifteen vendors at their wedding, including florists, caterers, band or disc jockey, photographer, baker, and so on. You will be spending money on the venue, invitations, favors, transportation, and more. How many vendors are *you* using? What if you "borrowed" a little money from each vendor or portion of your budget? What if you bought in-season flowers to save money; eliminated an appetizer or chafing dish at the cocktail hour; or thought twice about how much you wanted to spend on favors in order to save money? By doing this, you may save yourself thousands of dollars to put toward the gown of your dreams.

RANDY RULE #5

You can always purchase
a cheaper dress, but
in the end it will be only
the price that you love.

The moment
Shannon stepped
into this gown,
she knew it was
the one.

Now, please understand me: I know the dress won't always be the number one budget priority. If you come from a family that loves to eat, you may want to spend more money on a huge family feast than you want to spend on your dress. If you are a music lover who loves to dance, you'll probably want to spend more money on a band or DJ. You are the only one who truly knows how much you can comfortably afford or how much you wish to spend.

Remember that big moment I described in the last chapter, the moment in the ceremony when the celebrant says, "I now pronounce you husband and wife"? You don't want to hear: "I now pronounce you...in massive debt," do you? No! I don't want that, either!

But I do want you to have and wear the dress of your dreams. As long as you stay within the overall *wedding* budget you've established, you should be able to do this. Remember that a wedding dress is worn once, but photographed *forever*.

SHANNON AND RAY'S STORY

Shannon is a former Miss Florida USA and cheerleader for the Miami Dolphins. If Shannon is used to anything, it's trying on and wearing glitzy gowns. When it came time to buy her wedding gown, she figured it would be the same old, same old. But she didn't count on how surprising it would feel to put on the right dress that embodied her true story.

Shannon had the good fortune to "win" a wedding dress. She had been selected by a design house as the winner of a national contest where she was awarded $3,000 toward the purchase of a dress and two round-trip tickets to New York. She first visited the designer's salon and narrowed her selection to two dresses, including a gown that with the prize money would have cost her very little.

However, Shannon decided to visit Kleinfeld, where she found *the* dress—the dress she would ultimately purchase at full price because it was just...well, right. The dress had a dramatic jewel-encrusted V-neckline that proudly showed off her bust and shoulders. "It was the wow dress," Shannon said. "It had the perfect combination of sexy and sparkle—and most important, it did not look like a pageant dress."

Shannon had often regretted a choice she made while she was Miss Florida USA. At her most important competition, she opted for a dress she could afford, rather than figuring out a budget to pay for a dress she really wanted. She didn't want to make that mistake a second time.

On her wedding day, Shannon was determined to get the dress that felt right. She focused on her fiancé, Ray.

"Unlike all the years I competed and all the gowns I had worn, this dress, this day was about me and Ray, not about how many points I could get. I wasn't trying to win anything. I'd already won him. I wanted the dress to give him everything he wanted."

SAMPLE SALES

Is there any way to afford a designer wedding dress on a more modest budget? Yes, you can shop for a wedding gown at a salon sample sale. However, sample sales aren't for everyone. You need to be in the right frame of mind to shop one.

A Few Facts and Pointers

• Most salons host sample sales at least twice a year. Check with your salon for their schedule. Inventory is liquidated, and you can get last season's dresses and floor samples at much lower prices—sometimes even as much as 80 percent off the original price.

• Before a sample sale, you need to check out the selection of dresses so you know which ones you might want to purchase before the sale begins. Bring along a couple of photographs of gowns that you love. Even if these gowns aren't on sale, the salon or your consultant may be able to guide you to a similar-looking gown style. Sample sales can be hit or miss, so be sure to manage your expectations about what you may or may not find. There will also be other brides in the salon who may be reaching for the same dress at the same time! You need to be prepared for anything.

• Women who are a bridal size 8 or 10 will have the best luck at these sales, since most samples are carried in those sizes (thus the name *sample sale*). Keep in mind that if you're a fuller-figured bride, you will probably have less luck finding a sample dress that will fit you. Contact the salon in advance to see if they'll have any plus-size dresses on sale.

• You will have to arrive very early and most likely wait on line before the store even opens.

• When your bridal consultant asks the all-important question, "How much would you like to spend?" don't dodge the question! Please be honest! It will save you a lot of time and heartache in the dressing room.

• You need to be prepared to make an instant decision to purchase a dress. If you're the kind of person who needs time to make a decision, or if you're the kind of bride who needs an hour-and-a-half consultation and a private fitting room, a sample sale may not be right for you.

Don't forget that sample sale dresses are sold "as is" and won't necessarily be in perfect condition. They will most likely need cleaning and require some minor repair. Some of the beading may

When you're with the right consultant, she should be able to help you find the perfect dress at *any* budget.

A sample sale can be a way to find a beautiful gown at a great price.

have fallen off and will need to be replaced. And remember, as with all gowns, you will need alterations! Some salons won't do alterations on sale dresses. When you think of the "bargain" factor, make sure you've figured in the costs for these likelihoods to be sure you are actually getting a bargain. If you're a sample-size bargain shopper, however, then a sample sale may be just the right opportunity for you.

When you're with the right consultant, she should be able to help you find the perfect dress at *any* budget. The consultant shouldn't refuse any request from you without a clear explanation. A good consultant should also give you options and alternatives that will help you make your vision come to life at the right cost for you.

Decide on the Season and Time of Day

The date or season of the year can greatly affect your choice of wedding gown. Some styles and fabrics can be ruled out simply by virtue of the fact that they aren't necessarily friendly to certain times of year or day. If you make up your mind about these things *before* you shop for a dress, I promise it will help make your dress decision easier.

In a perfect world, there's a timeline I'd suggest for finding, trying on, and purchasing your wedding dress. Of course, there will be weddings that get planned sooner than this, and many that get planned at the last minute. Use my timeline as a basic guide to how long things *typically* take.

In general, it takes around six to eight months for a dress to be ordered and delivered to a salon. You need to work around that time frame, factoring the *extra* time you will need to find accessories and get alterations. And take note: If your dress-purchasing schedule is accelerated, you will probably have to pay more for certain things due to rush charges.

Once you have chosen that all-important date for your wedding, the process really kicks into high gear. That's when your timeline starts.

Here are some questions you should ask yourself:

• What season are you planning to have your wedding: spring, summer, fall, or winter? Choose fabrics accordingly. See page 62.

• What time of day will the wedding take place? Morning, afternoon, or evening?

• Are you planning your wedding around a sentimental or important date?

• Have you considered the convenience of the date you're choosing for guests?

• Have you considered having your wedding on a less desirable day, like the middle of the week or a Friday or Sunday? (Keep in mind that this may be another way to help you cut back costs.)

• If you're having your wedding outdoors, you may want to consider what time the sun will be setting. How will this affect the temperature? Will your guests be blinded by the sun and not able to see your nuptials?

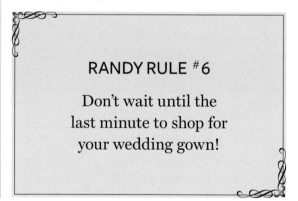

RANDY RULE #6

Don't wait until the last minute to shop for your wedding gown!

Clockwise from left: Shannon, Allison, Crystal, and Jennifer. Each chose a wedding gown perfect for the season and time of day of her wedding.

12+ MONTHS BEFORE

- Define your story.
- Imagine your dress.
- Establish a budget.
- Choose a date and time.
- This is when the five essentials take shape:

  *Your Story, Your Plan, Your Gown,
  Your Body, Your Look*

8–12 MONTHS BEFORE

- Your bridal appointment needs
  to be scheduled.
- Begin shopping for your gown.
- Begin shopping for bridesmaids' dresses.

6–8 MONTHS BEFORE

- This is the ideal deadline for making
  your big decision and ordering your
  wedding dress.

  Note: If you order your wedding gown
  less than six months before your wedding,
  you may incur rush charges and may
  not be able to order certain styles or
  from some designers.

- Shop for your headpiece, veil, shoes,
  and other accessories.

- Begin deciding what your groom is going to wear.
  He may want to start shopping for his attire.

- Decide upon bridesmaids' outfits, since these will
  need time for alterations as well. See page 188 for
  more information.

4–6 MONTHS BEFORE

- You should have all of your accessories purchased
  by this time. Most veils and accessories take
  around four months to order.

- You should decide on a hairstyle. Make sure it
  works with your headpiece and veil.

- Your groom should have his suit or tux ordered
  by now.

- Your groom should start shopping for tie, pocket
  square, socks, shoes, and any other accessories he
  will wear to the wedding.

- Make sure the mothers of the bride and groom are
  shopping for their appropriate outfits, too.

6–8 WEEKS BEFORE

• Your gown should have arrived at the salon!

Note: If you haven't heard from your salon by now about your gown, I would contact them and check on the delivery date.

• Once the dress comes in and goes through quality control, your salon should contact you to set up your first fitting appointment.

• Consider your makeup. If someone is doing it for you, now's the time for a trial run.

4 WEEKS BEFORE

• Schedule your fittings. You need to coordinate with your salon on how many fittings you will need.

• Bridesmaids, mothers, your groom, and all other members of the bridal party need to have their garments, shoes, and accessories by now.

2 WEEKS BEFORE

• This is when you should have your third or possibly final fitting.

• You may want to have a final trial run with your hairstylist and makeup artist.

• Take photos. Some brides schedule their hair appointment before their fitting appointment so they can see their hairstyle with the dress.

• If you need a final trim for your hair, do it now.

• Gather all the items you will need for your wedding day.

• Schedule your manicure and pedicure.

• Schedule the date to pick up your dress.

1 WEEK BEFORE

• Make sure you have your gown and all your accessories.

• Memorize your vows.

• Take time for manicure, pedicure, facial, and treat yourself to a massage—you've earned it.

In chapter 10, I have some critical step-by-step details about getting ready and making the "big day" a big success.

Choose Your Location

Figuring out your wedding location actually goes hand in hand with selecting a wedding dress. It's important that your wedding dress and your venue are telling the *same* story.

You may want a different dress style or fabric to work with a particular place, whether indoors or outdoors. If your location is very intimate, for instance, you may want to choose a dress with a slimmer silhouette, or reconsider purchasing a gown with an enormous train. If you decide to host a destination wedding, there will be different questions and considerations depending on the specific site. Will your destination wedding be held on a beach in the Caribbean, at a vineyard in California, or on the ski slopes in Colorado? Who knows, your destination may be in Europe or even in a barn at your grandparents' farm!

> If you decide to host a destination wedding, there will be different questions and considerations depending on the specific site.

For example, if you choose a heavy satin beaded gown but then decide to wed in Aruba...can you really handle the heat in the fabric you've selected? Or vice versa: Do you really see yourself getting married in organza in the middle of winter in Colorado?

Keep in mind: I'm not saying you *can't* have satin in Aruba or organza in the winter. I want you to have *whatever* you desire. I saw a wedding on the beach in the Caribbean where the bride wore a silk satin gown, and she looked stunning.

These questions will help you narrow down your choice of venues, and they'll also point you toward the kind of dress you want to purchase:

- How does the location affect the style or fabric of your dress?
- Where will you host your ceremony?
- Where will you host your reception?
- Is your location indoors or outdoors?
- If your location is outdoors, do you have a back-up plan for bad weather?
- How does the size of the location affect the size and style of your dress?
- Are you having a destination wedding?
- How will you transport your dress?
- Is it easy to access your location and convenient for you and your guests?
- Are there hotels or places to stay that are convenient for you and your guests and at different price points?
- Does your location reflect your story?
- Is your venue within your budget?

Jessica wanted a gown with a vintage look, which fit in perfectly with the period ball-room where her reception was held.

I once worked with a bride who became completely frustrated because she simply couldn't find a gown that she liked. She was getting married in a barn and decided to choose a gown that she considered appropriate for the location: something deconstructed and relaxed. She was trying on dresses with a casual elegant look. When I asked her what kind of gown she had always pictured herself wearing, she said she had always wanted a sparkling, beaded gown. I went to the stockroom and pulled a Monique Lhuillier gown with a solid-crystal-encrusted bodice, a silk satin-organza skirt with "pickups," and a matching crystal beaded bolero jacket. She put it on and burst into tears. "I love this gown!" she exclaimed. I told her, "Then you should wear it." She bought the gown and hung a crystal chandelier in the middle of the barn and everything was perfect!

I love this story and have many that are similar. I will suggest, however, that factors like your location, temperature, weather, and time of day should be taken into consideration to ensure your comfort and overall happiness on your wedding day.

Once you have figured out your budget, date, and location, you've made several of the key decisions needed to plan your wedding successfully. But incredibly, we've barely scratched the surface of our planning process!

There are thousands of dresses out there. Now we need even more ways for you to narrow down your selection. How will we do it?

The next thing that will help you find the right dress for you is to first understand the basics of bridal gown construction. Not only will I teach you some dress terminology, which will help when speaking with your consultant, but you will also become familiar with the wide range of dress silhouettes and fabrics that will work perfectly with your story.

Factors like your location, temperature, weather, and time of day should be taken into consideration to ensure your comfort and overall happiness on your wedding day.

Randy's Recap

DON'T WAIT UNTIL THE LAST MOMENT TO SHOP
FOR YOUR WEDDING GOWN

•

DECIDE ON THESE KEY THINGS BEFORE YOU
START SHOPPING FOR YOUR DRESS:

1. ESTABLISH A BUDGET

2. CHOOSE A DATE

3. CHOOSE YOUR LOCATION
AND TIME OF DAY

•

USE THE TIMELINE OFTEN
TO MAKE SURE YOU HAVEN'T FORGOTTEN
ANYTHING AS YOU GO

BRIANNE AND JESSE'S *STORY*

Hometown	Coram, New York
Wedding Date	September 10
Location	Gurney's Inn, Montauk—the beach!
Wedding Guests	160
Dress Designer	Lazaro

It's hard to believe that a wedding dress destiny could have been set so many years ago, but for these young, aspiring actors, true love began in the ninth grade, when Jesse left a carnation on Brianne's chair in school.

Jesse's wedding proposal included a scavenger hunt with notes leading the bride-to-be from one special location to the next, including their school, an old movie theater where they had their first kiss, and finally the beach. In the sand, Jesse had made a heart out of rocks and literally made Brianne dig her engagement ring out of a treasure chest. Then the horses arrived and they rode away on the beach together. This is a true story. So, really, there was no other dress for this bride except one that reflected all the parts of their story: beach, ocean, and the most incredible romantic gesture Brianne could have hoped for, the proposal. Their relationship was all about the beach!

After the consultant pulled out a few dresses, the perfect one was obvious. It took Brianne, along with her mom, sister, and best friend, only a short time to decide upon the dress: the one with the mermaid silhouette and the ruffles flowing on the train that looked just like ocean waves. "Randy saw me trying on the dress and gave it his seal of approval, but not before placing the veil on top of my head. He provided the finishing touch. He knew exactly what would make me feel like the perfect bride."

The beautiful turquoise earrings that Brianne wore coordinated perfectly with the gorgeous blue colors of the ocean and complemented her auburn locks.

Brianne's gown was perfect for her wedding on the beach.

CHAPTER THREE

YOUR *GOWN*
(Deconstructed)

A wedding dress really is the sum of its parts

Most women have some idea of what they want to look like on their wedding day, whether or not they've found the exact dress yet. Women come into the salon with photographs of the dresses they want to see. I can often tell where a bride's story is headed just by looking at these photographs. I get a "feeling" from what the bride shows me. Even if a bride isn't saying, "This is my story," she's giving me insight and clues to her story.

I don't want to overwhelm you with an encyclopedia of bridal terminology and definitions. I want to give you the basic words or "language" you will need to help navigate your way through this process with as little stress and anxiety as possible. Today's bride is busy and doesn't have the time it takes to learn *everything* about a wedding dress. However, a little knowledge and a few key words can be a powerful tool when looking for the right wedding gown! And brides who come into the salon *prepared* do much better in finding their perfect dress.

The Gown

Anytime you try on a new dress, consider these components separately and together. First, observe how a dress looks on the hanger; then pay attention to how it looks on you. Though there are many elements that help make wedding dresses unique, these are the basic parts of a dress you should know:

Silhouette
The shape of the dress. The shape of the skirt helps define it.

Front neckline
The top of the bodice, which defines your upper body and helps to frame your face, neck, and shoulders.

Back neckline
The back of the bodice, which defines your back, neck, and shoulders.

Bodice
The bodice shapes your bust, waist, and hips.

Sleeves
Sleeves cover your arms.

Waistline
How a dress fits in relation to your natural waistline.

Hemline
The bottom edge, or length of the dress.

Petticoat or Crinoline
The fabric or foundation that's used under a skirt to help hold its shape or silhouette.

Train
The length of the back of the skirt.

Bustle
How a train is picked up.

The other facets of a wedding gown that can make it special are the fabric, lace, and embellishments. Read on to learn more about these elements.

Charmaine's beaded lace gown features a strapless bodice, an empire waist, and a slim fit-to-flare silhouette.

SILHOUETTE

Though there are many variations on wedding dress silhouettes worn by brides, these are the ones I consider the most popular, and the silhouettes that I feel you should know.

A-LINE

This silhouette refers to a gown that resembles the letter A. (The shape of the skirt in this silhouette can vary from slim to full.) This silhouette is probably the most popular and works for almost any body shape.

BALL GOWN

A gown with a dramatically full skirt that typically has a natural or dropped waist.

FIT-TO-FLARE

Also known as the modified A-line, this shape is fitted to the upper thighs, and then gently flares out at the bottom. It's fitted more closely than an A-line, but flares out more gently than a mermaid or trumpet.

MERMAID

A fitted gown with a seam above the knee that flares out with a very full bottom.

SHEATH

A slim gown that hugs the body with a straight shape.

TRUMPET

A fitted gown that is similar to a mermaid, but gently flares out at the bottom. Its gentle flare is usually made with princess seams instead of the seam above the knee.

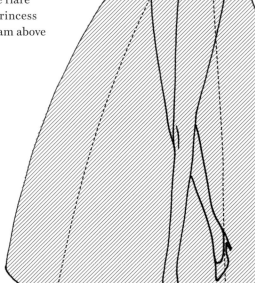

Illustration of an A-line silhouette with princess seams.

PRINCESS SEAMS

Princess is a term that people often confuse with the shape of the dress, but it actually refers to vertical seams on a dress and not necessarily the silhouette. You can have princess seams on almost any of the dress silhouettes.

A-LINE
      BALL GOWN
      FIT-TO-FLARE

MERMAID
      SHEATH
      TRUMPET

FRONT NECKLINE

The front neckline is a key element on your dress because it frames your upper body and your face. Trust me, when you prepare to walk down that aisle, all eyes will be on your face, so you want it framed perfectly! Some key necklines you should know:

BATEAU OR SABRINA

A neckline that is open from shoulder to shoulder and follows the line of your collarbone. The term *Sabrina* was coined when actress Audrey Hepburn wore this neckline in the movie *Sabrina*. Also sometimes called a boat neckline.

HALTER

A sleeveless neckline that wraps around the neck.

HIGH-NECK

The fabric goes up and covers part of your neck in a mandarin collar or turtleneck.

JEWEL

A round neckline that rests at the base of the neck.

OFF-THE-SHOULDER

This neckline falls off the shoulders and wraps around your arms. (It can have a V-neck, scoop neck, square neck, sweetheart, or others.) It doesn't allow for the full range of motion of your arms. Consider how you will dance with your groom or toss your bouquet.

ON-THE-SHOULDER

This neckline has fabric that rests on the shoulder. It can feature different shapes, for example V-neck, scoop neck, square neck, sweetheart, and so on.

STRAPLESS

A bodice that has no sleeves. It can be straight across, dipped, sweetheart, or even raised.

TIP-OF-THE-SHOULDER

The top of the gown rests at the tips of your shoulders. It can have different shapes, such as V-neck, scoop neck, square neck, sweetheart, and the like.

Now, I realize that there are several dozen more necklines and variations that you might see on dresses in a salon. I know there are brides out there thinking, "Why don't you tell me everything, Randy! I want to know every neckline!" This is a perfect example of my point about getting overwhelmed with information. Knowing twenty different necklines and silhouettes is not really going to bring you closer to your ideal dress.

The dress I designed for that bridal contest at FIT, my first wedding gown (see page 6), was a halter-style gown, which was considered radical at that time. I actually hadn't been to many weddings, so I didn't know there was a rule about covering your shoulders and not wearing halters. But guess what? I broke that rule, and now halter dresses are not uncommon.

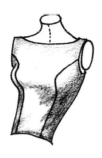

BATEAU

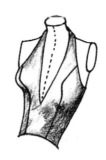

HALTER

HIGH-NECK

JEWEL

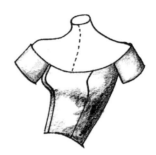

OFF-THE-SHOULDER

ON-THE-SHOULDER

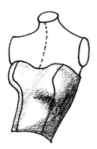

STRAPLESS

TIP-OF-THE-SHOULDER

BACK NECKLINE

Many brides love to show off their backs! This is a great way to give a little exposure and be a bit sexy without being too risqué. You can choose a keyhole back, a scoop, or a very low or plunging back. If you want to show less skin, you can have a lace panel that gives a peek-a-boo effect. If you have a gorgeous back and want to show it off, I say go for it! Just remember that if you want a really low back, the neckline needs to be on the shoulder. A strapless dress can only be lowered so far in the back, because the bodice will need support. How low will you go?

KEYHOLE

A keyhole back refers to an opening in the back of the bodice. It is usually in a circle, oval, or teardrop shape.

SCOOP

A scoop back is U-shaped. It can be high or very low.

STRAPLESS

A strapless back can have several variations, for example: straight across, a slight dip, or a slight V-shape. A strapless bodice cannot be lowered too much because it needs support to keep it up.

V-BACK

Is in the shape of the letter V. It can be a slight V or a very deep V.

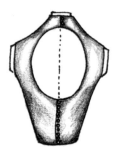
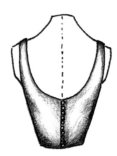
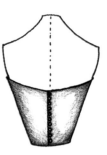
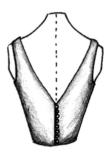

KEYHOLE   SCOOP   STRAPLESS   V-BACK

WHY ARE THERE SO MANY STRAPLESS DRESSES?

This is a question I get asked a lot. The main reason is because women do not like to be restricted in their gowns. Any fitted gown with a sleeve will restrict your movement. Most brides want to be able to raise their arms to dance at their reception and be able to toss their bouquets easily. Both society and religions have also become less strict about what you can wear for weddings, and a more relaxed culture has allowed for more exposure of skin.

If you have religious requirements where sleeves are needed, or you're a modest bride who doesn't feel comfortable with exposing her arms, you can still go strapless without worry. Designers have invented shrugs, boleros, wraps, and other cover-ups for brides like you!

BODICE

The bodice is the part of your dress, between the neckline and the skirt, structured around your torso. The neckline and the waist help to define the bodice.

Take note: Your bodice is the top of the dress and near your face. It will be highly featured in your wedding photographs and portraits. You should pay close attention to the details of your bodice. How does it frame your face and shape your waist?

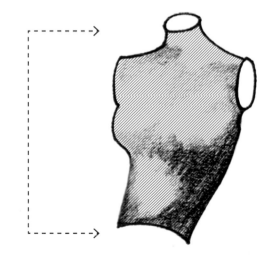

Brooke fell in love with her sheer jeweled sleeves.

SLEEVES

Yes, most dresses in bridal salons are strapless. But there are dresses with sleeves, too! If you want to wear sleeves, keep in mind that you don't need to know every single type of sleeve. There are many variations on sleeves, including angel, bell, bishop, cap, circular, dolman, fitted, gathered, kimono, puffed, raglan, trumpet…the list goes on!

Again, you don't need to learn them all. Stick to the basics and keep it simple. What shape and length of sleeve looks best on you: cap, short, three-quarter, or long? Take a look at different sleeve shapes and lengths and ask yourself: Which is most flattering on you?

Take a look at different sleeve shapes and lengths
and ask yourself: Which is most flattering on you?

BROOKE'S STORY

Brooke told me she wanted a gown with sleeves. I didn't want her to look too covered up, so I pulled this Badgley Mischka gown for her with sheer sleeves that have exquisite crystals and beading on them. Even though she told me she didn't like beading, I asked her to try it. I knew she would love it.

"I would never in a million years have worn sleeves with beading! It just sounded terrible somehow. But it was far from terrible. It was gorgeous! Then Randy placed a jeweled headpiece on me with even more sparkling crystals and beads. I felt like the dress and all this sparkle was expressing a different part of my personality that I hadn't considered. I'm just not into lots of embellishments like beads and crystals, yet here I stood in glittering jewels, and I loved it!"

WAISTLINE

Your natural waistline is usually located right at your navel. The waistline of a gown generally refers to the skinniest part of the bodice. It can also refer to a horizontal seam that separates the bodice of the dress from the skirt. Although there are many variations, wedding gowns tend to have a few key waistline styles.

NATURAL

This falls right at your natural waist.

DROPPED

This falls below your natural waist. It can be shaped straight across, into a V-shape called a Basque waist, scoop, square, or even inverted.

EMPIRE

This is a high waist. It is above your natural waist and usually falls right under your bust.

PRINCESS

Princess refers to the vertical seams that shape the bust and waist. It has no horizontal waist seam.

HEMLINE

Based on the silhouette you choose, hemlines and skirt lengths are fairly standard. There are quite a few in-between lengths, but basically they are either long or short.

The length of your gown generally tells your guests how formal your wedding will be. Gowns that touch the floor are the most formal; dresses that fall from mid-calf to ankle are considered semi-formal. Short dresses are typically informal. Here is the breakdown of hemlines:

SHORT

A dress whose hem ends above the knee. It can be a mini, mid-thigh, or just above the knee.

MEDIUM

A dress that falls below the knee. Variations include below the knee, ballet, and tea-length.

LONG

A long gown almost skims the floor.

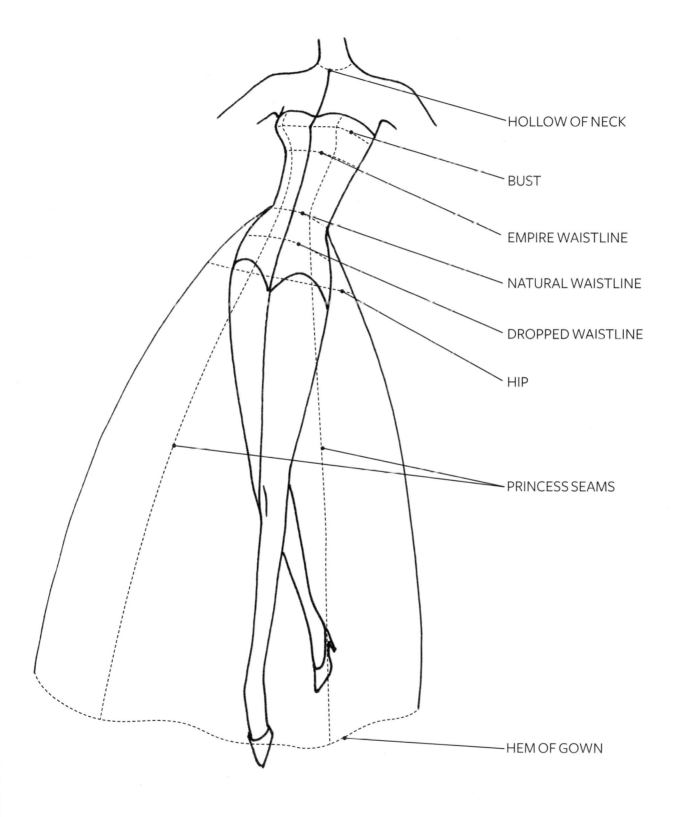

HOLLOW OF NECK

BUST

EMPIRE WAISTLINE

NATURAL WAISTLINE

DROPPED WAISTLINE

HIP

PRINCESS SEAMS

HEM OF GOWN

The petticoat under Jennifer's skirt is what helps it keep its A-line shape.

PETTICOAT OR CRINOLINE

This is the fabric or stiff foundation that's used under a skirt to help hold its shape or silhouette. It is typically made up of layers of stiff netting or crinoline.

Most petticoats are sewn into the dress, but if you want your skirt to be fuller, you can easily add an extra petticoat or crinoline underneath to make it more voluminous, or remove some of the netting during alterations to make your skirt less full. (See the alterations chapter, page 175.)

If you want your skirt to be fuller, you can easily add an extra petticoat or crinoline underneath to make it more voluminous.

REBECCA'S STORY

My girlfriend Rebecca was completely infatuated with bows. For every birthday or holiday I would buy her something with a bow on it, like a box or bow earrings from Tiffany's. So when she decided to choose her wedding gown, we knew we were looking for a gown with bows.

However, when Rebecca tried on dresses with bows, they simply looked silly on her. We were both a little disappointed that we couldn't find a dress for her with bows on it that she loved. I was designing at the time and chose to custom-design two dresses for Rebecca's wedding day. The first gown, for her ceremony, was a simple silk satin A-line gown with a heavily beaded neckline. The second dress, for her reception, had a boned corset-bodice with a full tulle ball gown skirt. Without telling Rebecca, I had my seamstresses sew literally hundreds and hundreds of satin-trimmed white organza bows on her petticoat. On her wedding day, Rebecca's face lit up when I lifted her tulle skirt and showed her all of the bows we had sewn on. It ended up being a highlight of her reception. Everyone laughed throughout the night when she lifted her skirt crying out, *"I GOT MY BOWS!"* We were all happy that one of the most important parts of *her* story was included within her dress!

TRAIN

The train is the fabric that rests on the floor in the back of the gown's skirt. It is a great way to give a gown a dramatic look when walking down the aisle. Don't forget that guests will be looking at your back during most of your ceremony. When you consider how long you want the train of your gown, you must consider the place where you're getting married. How and where will you adjust the dress for your reception? Trains must be bustled carefully, so you will need to assign someone to be your official "bustler." Generally, I don't recommend a train on a tulle gown because it looks bulky when it's bustled. For a tulle gown, consider either wearing a long veil or having a separate train that's detachable. Your train will be bustled for your reception, so be sure your gown looks good bustled!

There are several lengths of train you need to know. The real question you need to ask yourself is, "How long will I go?"

I will never forget one very special bride who was confined to a wheelchair.

When she got engaged, she knew she wanted to have a wedding dress with a train. We ordered extra fabric from the designer of her dress and created a one-of-a-kind train that slipped over the back of her chair and trailed behind her. Everyone at the salon was anxious when we tested it for the first time. Would the wheels roll over the fabric? When she turned around, it worked perfectly! When she rolled down the aisle on her wedding day, with the train attached to the back of her wheelchair, everyone stayed seated so friends and family could see the bride and her train.

Examples of different trains.

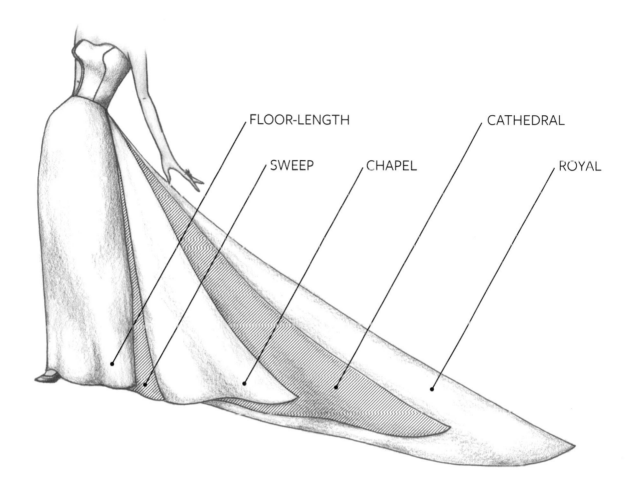

FLOOR-LENGTH

SWEEP   CHAPEL

CATHEDRAL

ROYAL

FLOOR-LENGTH

This gown has no train.

SWEEP

A short train that extends a foot or less from where the hem hits the floor.

CHAPEL

A mid-length train that extends about two to three feet on the floor.

CATHEDRAL

A long train that extends three or more feet on the floor.

ROYAL OR MONARCH

A very long train that extends from six to nine feet or more. You should be tall, have a very long aisle, and have an ultra-formal wedding for this!

WATTEAU

A train that falls from the shoulders. This train can be any length.

DETACHABLE

Any train that can be removed or detached.

BUSTLE

A bustle is created when the fabric from the train of your dress gets pulled up in the back so the hem becomes floor-length. A bustle allows you to walk around comfortably and dance during your reception without stepping on the fabric from your train. A train can get bustled with hooks and eyes, with buttons and loops, or with ribbons. These are sewn onto the dress so that the train can be lifted up. Don't forget that if your dress has a heavy train, once it's bustled, you'll be carrying that heavy train around all night.

When it comes to the job of bustling, you really do have to practice. The person who will be bustling your dress should accompany you to at least one fitting so they can become familiar with the dress and learn how to properly bustle. You should also have a backup plan in case a ribbon breaks or a button pops. Trust me! You should have a repair kit handy.

FRENCH BUSTLE

The train is pulled under the back of the skirt and attached with ribbons or buttons and loops. Depending on the gown, this is my favorite bustle. It adds a bit of drama to the back, and if placed low will not add bulk to your backside.

HEM BUSTLE

The hem of the train is brought up and attached underneath the skirt with ribbons or buttons and loops. This makes the back of the gown floor-length and creates a "bubble hem" effect.

TRADITIONAL BUSTLE

The fabric from the train is pulled over the skirt and attached with buttons and loops or hooks and eyes.

Anna's French bustle will allow her to walk and dance comfortably at her reception.

Fabric

Choosing the fabric of a dress is all about what kind of weight, texture, drape, and formality you want from your wedding dress. There are so many fabric choices, I could literally fill an entire book simply with different types!

I've come up with some basics that I think will help you to understand fabric better. Ultimately, you want to choose a fabric that flatters you and makes you feel good. It should also be appropriate for the formality, season, and setting of your wedding.

Fabric versus Fiber

Let me clear up some confusion between *fabric* and *fiber*. Brides come to me all the time and say, "I want a gown made of a silk fabric." When they say this, I know they usually mean satin. Silk is a fiber, not a fabric. So are wool, rayon, cotton, and nylon. Fabric is created when these fibers are woven and finished into a particular material. Silk can be woven and finished to create many different fabrics, including satin, organza, taffeta, mikado, and even velvet.

> ## You want to choose a fabric that flatters you and makes you feel good.

Silk versus Synthetic

Many wedding gowns are made of silk, but many are not. Most people outside the fashion industry can't easily tell the difference between a silk fabric and one that's made from a synthetic. Because I've spent many years studying and designing fashion, I can spot a synthetic fabric easily. Okay, I have to confess. Ladies, I am a bit of a fabric snob. I would prefer a bride wear a simple gown that is made of a beautiful silk fabric rather than a very ornate gown made of a synthetic one. That's not to say that there aren't great synthetic fabrics and gowns out there. I simply love the way silk drapes and feels to the touch.

So what's the difference? Silk is a natural fiber obtained from the cocoons of the silkworm. A synthetic is a man-made fiber like nylon, rayon, or acetate. Today there are more synthetic alternatives to silk that look great! A synthetic fabric may actually be a more cost-effective and durable choice for you.

Also know that sometimes even though a dress says it's made of "silk," it may be a blend of silk and polyester. Fabric designers often use polyester to stabilize silk so the resulting fabric is stronger and has fewer imperfections.

How can you tell the difference between the two? One telltale sign of a synthetic fabric is its color. Because silk is a natural fiber, it can only be bleached to a certain shade of white. Synthetic fabrics, like rayon, nylon, and acetate, can come in a stark white color. I suggest that if you *do* go with a synthetic fabric, consider a shade that is not that ghastly white color but instead an off-white, ivory, or diamond white that will look richer. As a general rule, only someone with a dark or olive skin tone looks best in stark white.

FABRICS YOU NEED TO KNOW

BROCADE

A thick, heavy, jacquard-woven fabric with raised designs, most often featuring a floral pattern. Typically worn for winter weddings.

CHARMEUSE

A shiny, lightweight fabric with a very soft drape. It is usually used for sexy, slinky dresses and often cut on the bias to hug every curve of your body. Think of the movie stars from the 1930s.

CHIFFON

A delicate, transparent, and sheer fabric made from silk or polyester. It is often layered, gathered, draped, or used for sheer sleeves. When you think of chiffon, think of a Greek goddess.

CREPE

A medium-weight fabric with a matte, slightly coarse finish. It drapes softly and, like charmeuse, clings closely to the body.

FAILLE (pronounced *file*)

A medium-weight fabric that can be slightly stiff with a low luster. Its main characteristic is its tiny raised ribs, which are similar to but finer than a grosgrain ribbon.

GAZAR

A loosely woven fabric with a low luster. It looks like a thick, dense organza with a crisp finish, and is very buoyant.

LACE

See page 68.

MIKADO

A heavier-weight twill-weave fabric with a medium luster. Because of its body, it's great for making architectural gowns.

ORGANZA

A very lightweight, plain-woven, sheer, and crisp fabric. Can be made from silk, rayon, polyester, or nylon.

SATIN

One of the most common fabrics used for wedding gowns. It is densely woven and typically lustrous on one side, dull on the other. It can be made of acetate, polyester, or silk. It comes in different weights, duchesse satin being the heaviest.

SATIN-ORGANZA

A medium- to lightweight fabric with a sheen on the front and matte finish on the back. It looks like a cross between a satin and an organza with a buoyant finish. It can show wrinkles easily.

SHANTUNG

A light-weight fabric that is semi-lustrous and usually made of raw silk. Its main characteristic is the tiny slubs of raw silk running through it. It was originally woven in Shantung, China. Also called dupioni when it's made in a heavier weight.

TAFFETA

A thin, crisp, lightweight fabric with a very fine rib. It is tightly woven and looks the same on both sides. It can make a very full wedding gown that is lightweight and is known for its distinctive rustling sound. Because it's so thin, it also gathers nicely.

TULLE (pronounced *tool*) OR ILLUSION

A delicate and very sheer, fine netting or mesh made from nylon, silk, or rayon. It is used for veils or can be gathered in many layers for a fluffy wedding gown skirt.

VELVET

A plush, thick fabric made of silk, polyester, rayon, or cotton; it has a soft, thick, short pile. Mostly worn for winter weddings.

SATIN-ORGANZA

VELVET

SATIN (POLY)

ORGANZA

FLORAL BROCADE

CHIFFON

SHANTUNG

DUPIONI

MIKADO

CREPE

TAFFETA

SATIN (SILK)

GAZAR

CHARMEUSE

FAILLE

BROCADE

TRY FABRICS ON

The material of your gown can make a dramatic difference in the way it looks, feels, and drapes. It can also help you express the overall look and mood you are trying to achieve for your wedding. You need to try fabrics in the same way that you're trying different dress silhouettes. Ask yourself: Does a particular fabric help tell your story? Does it fit in with your plan? Does it match the season, time of day, and formality of the wedding? Does the fabric look too white or shiny? Does it look too formal or too casual for your wedding?

Keep an open mind when trying on different fabrics. I've had many brides tell me they don't like a certain fabric, and then end up choosing a gown made of it. You may have said you'd never try a dress with lace, but that could change once you try it on.

There are lots of rules out there about which fabrics you're "supposed" to wear for the time of day and different seasons of the year. I have a different perspective. I believe you should choose a wedding dress mainly because you love it and it makes you feel beautiful! Now, I wouldn't recommend wearing a huge, heavy, satin ball gown on the beaches of Mexico in the middle of August. Although maybe *you* would! Keep in mind that many of these "rules" about what fabric to wear for a particular season were made *before* we had air-conditioning and heating.

Who's to say you *can't* head to a tropical island wearing a heavier satin dress? If you can handle the heat and you love the dress, then I say, "Go for it!" Sometimes a little air-conditioning can go a long way! Think about Pam, who got married at the Grand Canyon wearing a satin ball gown. The gown she wore was perfect for *her*!

So remember, before you make that final decision about your dress, make sure the fabric is right for you! It should help tell your story and fit in with your plan.

WHAT COLOR SHOULD I WEAR?

There are so many different shades of white you can choose from. And for all these variations on white, there are just as many names. You can really get confused! For example, one designer's "off-white" is another designer's "diamond white," "ivory," "ecru," "champagne," "vanilla," "candlelight," or "eggshell"! The list goes on! My point here is: Don't get hung up on the *name* of the color. Also, some dresses may only come in one color, while others may be offered in many different shades. The most important thing is that you choose a color that complements your skin tone. If you have a dark olive complexion, does a bright white look more flattering on you? Are you very pale, and pure white washes you out? Again, there are a lot of rules about what color you "should" wear for your particular skin tone. However, you should really hold a fabric color next to your skin to make this decision.

When choosing the color of your dress, also think about the lighting at your wedding. Bright sunlight and indoor lighting will look different on fabrics. Consider whether your light source is natural or artificial and how it will affect the look of your dress and accessories.

And keep in mind, brides: I believe you are

always allowed to wear white! There are no "Randy Rules" saying you can't wear white if you're a more mature bride, a bride who is celebrating her second marriage, or a bride who already has children. I will say I am a bit of a traditionalist and love a bride in white, but if getting married in a pale pink dress feels right to you, then you should do it!

Sometimes brides choose colored fabrics for their wedding dresses, especially if they celebrate traditions from other countries. Remember: It's your wedding; it's your story.

WILL MY DRESS WRINKLE?

This is a question every bride wants to know. The simple answer is *yes*! All fabrics will wrinkle. I would be wary of any salesperson who tells you your dress won't wrinkle. It is true that some fabrics don't wrinkle as easily. Lace doesn't show wrinkles; silk satin and many synthetic fabrics are better at resisting wrinkles. The fiber the fabric is made of, the way it's woven, and the way it's finished all determine how well it will ward off wrinkles. The simplest way to find out how easily your dress will wrinkle is to take some of its fabric in your hand, crumple it up, and then release it. Is it wrinkled, or does it spring back into shape?

REMOVING WRINKLES ON THE FLY

Once I went to a wedding where the bride invited me back to the room where she and her bridal party were dressing. When I walked in, she jumped to her feet to greet me.

When I looked at her, all I could see was a mass of wrinkles across the waist of her gown where she had been sitting. I thought to myself: Do I tell her that her gown is wrinkled and completely freak her out? Not a chance! As I walked toward her to give her a hug, I quickly scanned the room and spotted a steamer in the corner. After I finished hugging her and telling her how stunning she looked, I pointed to the steamer and calmly asked her if I could borrow it. "Of course," she said. I then filled it with water and plugged it in. Once it had heated up, I asked her if she would mind if I removed some of the wrinkles from the front of her dress. She looked down at her dress in complete shock, and for the first time saw the wrinkles. I spent the next few minutes with a towel and my hand up the front of her gown carefully removing all of the creases with the steamer. The whole time, I was thinking to myself: I just hope the groom doesn't walk in right about now. This may be a bit hard to explain! When I finished, she hugged and thanked me profusely. She walked down the aisle that evening wrinkle-free and gorgeous!

TIP: For getting out wrinkles on the fly, I recommend using the travel steamer by Rowenta. I always travel with mine and also pack along an extension cord (it seems the electrical outlet is never where you need it).

Lace

Lace is an ornamental openwork patterned fabric with open holes. It's usually made of cotton and features tiny "eyelashes" when it's cut off the loom. It's romantic, feminine, and synonymous with weddings. It's been around for centuries and is a staple in bridal dresses and veils.

True lace is created when threads are looped, twisted, or braided to other threads, separate from a backing fabric. Most fine lace is woven on looms in France. It can be used for an entire dress, or used as an accent trim or appliqué on a dress.

Corded or re-embroidered lace is heavier than Chantilly lace and can make a more prominent presence on a dress or veil. For me, there is nothing like a true French lace, which is made from cotton and has little or no sheen. However, some machine-made imitation laces are beautiful and can be a less expensive option as well. Don't rule them out.

There's a simple way to tell the difference between real and synthetic laces. If your lace has any kind of sheen, it is probably made from a synthetic fiber. Also, an imitation lace doesn't have the fine "eyelashes" that a real French lace has. These tiny threads running along the edges of lace are left when the lace has been cut from a loom.

> For me, there is nothing like a true French lace.

ALENÇON

The most popular lace, it originated in the town of Alençon, France. It usually features flowers or swirls that are outlined with a heavy silky cording on a net background. Can be used as an allover fabric or as appliqués.

CHANTILLY

A very delicate, lightweight lace usually made of a blend of rayon, cotton, or nylon. It has a fine mesh often featuring floral designs. It is flat—unlike re-embroidered Alençon lace, which has raised cording.

GUIPURE

A heavy raised lace with an open background, usually with large floral leafy patterns that are joined by threads. Can be used as an allover fabric or as appliqués.

POINT D'ESPRIT

A lightweight lace with dots woven on a mesh background.

From top to bottom: point d'esprit, guipure, Alençon, Chantilly.

Embellishments

Embellishments are to a dress what icing is to cake. That cake may be delicious, but it's the frosting that everyone sees first! There are numerous embellishments you can find on a wedding dress—including beading, appliqués, and trimmings—and they can completely change its look. Whether unadorned or ornately designed, the embellishments are the details of a dress that really make it come to life. Here are some of the most commonly used embellishments on wedding gowns:

Anna's beautifully embellished bodice.

APPLIQUÉS

BEADS

BOWS

BROOCHES

BUTTONS

CRYSTALS

EMBROIDERY

FEATHERS

FLOWERS

LACE

PEARLS

SEQUINS

Like building a house, constructing a dress is made up of many elements. It begins with a great foundation. Decide which silhouette and neckline are most flattering for you. Select a fabric and the right embellishments that work with your story and your plan.

From the top of its neckline to the bodice, all the way down to the hem and train of the dress, your gown should be a reflection of you and your personality. It should fit in with your story, and work with your plan. Your gown tells your guests your personal taste and style, and sets the tone for the rest of your wedding.

Randy's Recap

LEARN THE BASIC PARTS OF A WEDDING DRESS

•

FAMILIARIZE YOURSELF WITH DIFFERENT DRESS SILHOUETTES

•

CHOOSE THE SILHOUETTE AND NECKLINE THAT ARE
MOST FLATTERING TO YOU

•

GET TO KNOW YOUR FAVORITE FABRICS

•

MAKE SURE YOUR GOWN LOOKS BEAUTIFUL BUSTLED

•

WHEN CHOOSING YOUR GOWN, SELECT A COLOR THAT
COMPLEMENTS YOUR SKIN TONE

•

THE SILHOUETTE AND FABRIC, ALONG WITH LACE, CRYSTALS,
BEADING, AND OTHER EMBELLISHMENTS, CAN LEND GREAT DETAIL
TO YOUR WEDDING DRESS AND HELP TELL YOUR STORY

AMANDA AND GLENN'S *Story*

Hometown	New York City
Wedding Date	May 15
Location	Frick Collection, New York
Wedding Guests	150
Dress Designer	Carolina Herrera

Amanda and Glenn live in New York and are avid art lovers and collectors. Because they both live in a world of hectic schedules, they chose to plan their wedding in six short weeks, rather than wait another year or two. They set out to create an artistic wedding, at the Frick Collection, in a New York minute.

Amanda thought she had struck gold when she discovered a fashion spread of Carolina Herrera's wedding gowns in a bridal magazine and learned that each gown's design had been inspired by a famous painting! She thought, "This is our story, and our passion for art could be displayed in the gown I choose to wear." The couple fell in love with one particular gown inspired by a painting by Gustav Klimt. It was perfect! But finding the gown, a one-of-a-kind runway sample from Herrera's latest collection, would not be easy.

The couple persistently called and even visited Ms. Herrera's salon in hopes of ordering the gown. However, because the gown was so intricately designed with many layers of hand-cut tulle and hand beading, the masterpiece was not going into production, and therefore could not be ordered.

When I met Amanda and Glenn, they told me their story. I had just seen the dress on the runway at Herrera's bridal show and knew it was the perfect gown for Amanda! I called Herrera's office and confirmed that the gown was not being produced. Not about to give up, I asked if Amanda and Glenn could purchase the runway sample. Herrera agreed to sell the sample and send the gown over by messenger the very next day.

Now the question was: Would the gown fit? Although Amanda had a slender figure, the gown was a runway sample and had been sized to fit the model.

When Amanda stepped into the gown, everyone knew it was the dress! She looked like a work of art! After a few minor alterations, the runway sample fit her perfectly and, like a fine piece of art, had just found a place to be displayed.

Amanda's gown was a work of art, perfect for her museum reception.

CHAPTER FOUR

YOUR *B*ODY

*It's one thing to have a gorgeous dress;
it's another to have a gorgeous bride*

You've chosen a silhouette you'd like to wear, as well as the fabric, lace, and style of dress you love. Now what? You can know your story, make a plan, and learn all the facts about how dresses are constructed, but now you need to take another step forward and *relate* all that information to how dresses look on your body, to help you to find *your* perfect dress.

It's one thing to have a gorgeous dress; it's another thing to have a gorgeous bride. What makes a bride gorgeous is more than just a beautiful dress. A beautiful bride has self-confidence and doesn't let her dress overpower her *own* beauty. Make sure *you* wear the dress! On a hanger you may think you've got the ideal dress, but unless that dress looks and *feels* right on your body, it's just not right.

"Randy, what type of dress will be the most flattering for my body?" This is absolutely the number one question I get asked the most! It's the million-dollar question . . . and it's a trick question! I don't believe in labeling people or placing them in a group of predetermined shapes or sizes and then telling them what they should wear.

However, since this is the number one question brides have for me, I will give you my guidelines for choosing a dress that best flatters your body. Besides learning some general rules, it's a good starting point to know the basic shape of your body when shopping for clothes. What you need to know, however, is that every dress is cut and fits differently—and every body is shaped differently and therefore is unique!

So many articles, books, and even designers will present you with a neat, handy chart of body types. You know them—the ones where your body corresponds with a specific shape or fruit. This explains what you should wear if you're an hourglass, square, rectangle, pear, apple, watermelon, or whatever!

Well, here's what I have to say about all that information about what shape you are: Don't listen to it. Yes, ladies, you read that correctly.

Get it out of your head! Don't let anyone compare you to a fruit!

If I could do one thing for all brides, it would be to get them away from choosing their bridal gown style based on an arbitrary shape. It frustrates me that this is how women shop for a gown! They think they can look at a chart with pictures of shapes (which by the way don't look like most women I know) and make an intelligent decision about what dress they should wear!

RANDY RULE #7

Your body is not defined by a list of shapes.

Every day I meet brides who come to me with commentary about their own body shape:

"Well, Randy, I'm a pear shape, so I can only try on…"

"Well, I'm an inverted triangle, so should I avoid dresses that…"

"I have an hourglass figure, so I'll look good in…"

Here's why I want you to abolish these illogical ideas. A chart of body types will tell you, for instance, that your shape is "hourglass," and that you look good in one kind of dress. But how can you compare a woman who has an hourglass shape and who's five feet tall and 100 pounds to a woman who's over six feet tall and weighs 250 pounds? What if you're an "hourglass" and have a high waist? What if you're an "hourglass" and have a low waist? Don't you think a dress will fit differently on all these women—even though they

Checking how Shannon's gown falls.

are supposedly all similarly shaped? I will repeat: Every dress is cut and fits differently—and every body is unique and shaped differently!

Before making any decision about what type of dress is best for your body, consider these three words: *Try it on!*

I know that during the quest for the perfect wedding gown, it's important to pull out pictures of dresses you love. But please note: You can't choose any wedding dress solely from looking at a photograph or by looking at it on a hanger. That dress you think is just right in the magazine or in the store window may not work on your body. It doesn't matter if you're petite or tall, slim or plus-size, small-busted or large-busted. Whether you have a high waist, low waist, are straight or curvaceous…You still must *try it on!*

RANDY RULE #8

Never purchase a wedding dress without trying it on first.

GOWN SIZES

When you do try on that wedding gown, don't be alarmed if the sizing seems off. I know it's difficult to accept that even though you usually wear a size 10, in a wedding gown you will probably need a size 12 or 14. This is simply the way bridal gowns are sized. They are not true to the sizes of ready-to-wear clothes in your wardrobe. Even measurements may vary from one designer to another!

Most bridal salons have limited space and typically stock only one sample of each dress style. This "sample-size" wedding dress is usually a size 8 or 10 (which corresponds to a ready-to-wear 6 or 8). Of course, one size does not fit all. This is why, when you try on dresses at a bridal salon, a consultant clips the back of the dress: to give you an approximate idea of what your dress will look like when it is fitted to your body. Bridal sizing goes back to World War II when a sizing scale was used for making uniforms. Over time, sportswear adapted its sizes to reflect changing body shapes. Bridal gowns did not change. This is one reason why wedding gowns are typically two sizes bigger than the size you usually wear. Another reason bridal gowns seem to run small is because ready-to-wear clothing is made to fit your body more loosely and comfortably. Bridal gowns are meant to fit very close to your body. A bridal gown will probably be the most fitted garment you will ever wear.

Some salons may also carry a sampling of bridal gown styles in plus sizes for fuller-figured brides. Try not to get discouraged if you have to try on or even order your gown in a larger size than you're accustomed to.

Amanda was lucky enough to fit into this sample-size gown.

What Works Best on My Body?

This is what you've been waiting for. Instead of labeling you as one type of body shape, I'm going to break down the body into areas that I feel are the most important to consider when selecting your gown.

Most women want their bodies to be curvy, feminine, and shaped like an hourglass. Ideally, your bust, waist, and hips should all be in proportion to one another. As for dress shapes, an A-line gown works for almost any body shape. You generally can't go wrong there. However, there are more specific recommendations I will make.

The list that follows offers only *suggestions* for various parts of your body. Always remember that no matter what you think the right or wrong dress is for you, to be certain that it works for your specific body you still must…*try it on!*

Here are my recommendations regarding what to wear for your body, starting from the top and working our way down.

NECK

When it comes to a woman's neck, most want to achieve a longer, leaner appearance. Here are some suggestions on how to make your neck appear more elongated:

SHORT NECK

- V-necklines are a great way to visually lengthen the neck.

- A dipped or sweetheart neckline will make your neck appear longer and leaner.

- If your gown's neckline goes straight across, ask if either the designer or your seamstress can dip it for you. I recommend having this done during alterations so you can control the depth and shape of the dip. Sometimes the slightest dip can make a huge difference.

- Avoid big chunky necklaces that will make your neck appear shorter or visually cut it in half.

LONG NECK

- If you have a long neck, you are fairly lucky and will generally have more neckline options to choose from. You can wear a beautiful necklace if there isn't too much beading at the top of the bodice of your dress, which can look too glitzy.

- Wear a ruffled or high collar.

- Choose a Sabrina (also called a boat or bateau) neckline.

- Avoid deep plunging V-necklines or very deep sweethearts that will make your neck look even longer.

SHOULDERS

As a general rule, you want your shoulders to be in balance with your hips. They should be approximately the same width. Here is some advice to best show off your shoulders:

NARROW

- Try a tip-of-the-shoulder gown.

- Try an off-the-shoulder gown if you're okay with not being able to fully raise your arms.

- I would avoid wearing halters if you have narrow shoulders that are round. Halters can emphasize the fact that your shoulders are small.

AVERAGE

You can wear most necklines with average shoulders.

BROAD

- Try wearing an A-line or full skirt that will balance out your top.

- If you have nice square shoulders that aren't too broad, a halter neckline can emphasize their beauty. On the other hand, halters are not flattering if your shoulders are too broad or rounded.

- Avoid dresses that are straight. If you have broad shoulders, a too-straight gown will make you look like the letter T.

ARMS

Most women I meet have some insecurities or image issues with their arms. Some feel they are too masculine. Others believe their arms are not toned. And some women feel their arms are not in proportion. Some brides are not comfortable enough to go sleeveless or strapless. This can be challenging when searching for a wedding dress, since the majority of gowns today are strapless. Here are some recommendations for what to wear for different types of arms:

THIN

- If you want to make your arms appear larger, you can try covering them with a sleeve.

- If a sleeve can't be added to your gown, try wearing a bolero, jacket, or shrug.

- Try on an elegant pair of long gloves.

- Wear a coordinating wrap or stole.

- Avoid chunky bracelets that will make your arms look skinnier.

AVERAGE

You're in luck and can wear almost anything.

FULLER

- If you want to cover your arms, try a sleeve made of a light or sheer fabric that doesn't add bulk.

- Wear a sheer lace sleeve. Sometimes lace sleeves can look nice even when they are added to a solid fabric dress that doesn't have any lace on it.

- Go strapless. I know this goes against a lot of other people's rules, but I feel that bare arms can blend in with a bare neckline and call less attention to their size.

- Consider wearing a cap sleeve. You may be able to have your seamstress add this to your strapless gown.

- Wear a tip-of-the-shoulder gown. Even though it will give you a very small amount of coverage, it may visually look flattering and make you feel more comfortable.

- Avoid wearing sleeves that are too tight. If your sleeves are too tight, your arms will look like they've been stuffed into them.

- Don't wear sleeves made in a heavy fabric. This will only add bulk.

- I wouldn't recommend wearing a halter that draws attention to your arms.

- Don't wear gloves that end at the fullest part of your arms, making them appear even wider.

SHORT

- Strapless and halter necklines can be great for creating the illusion of longer arms.

- If you want to wear a bracelet, make it fine and delicate.

- Avoid short sleeves that will visually cut the length of your arm.

- Wearing gloves will create a horizontal line across your arms and make them appear shorter.

- Don't wear gloves with a gown that has sleeves!

LONG

- Consider wearing short or three-quarter-length sleeves.

- Try wearing a nice pair of gloves.

- Wear a bracelet that coordinates with your gown and accessories.

Susan wanted more coverage, so we added extra lace to create her cap sleeve.

Do I need to wear sleeves?

Sometimes fuller-figured brides with larger arms are told, "Don't go strapless. You *need* sleeves."

Some women have image issues with their arms and are told by "experts" or even members of their own family to cover them. Most believe a sleeve is a good solution. But think about it. Wrapping your arm in a fabric that is thick, heavy, or shiny will only make it look bigger. If the sleeve is loose, it will just add extra fabric and unnecessary bulk to your arm. If the sleeve is *too* tight, your arm can look like a stuffed sausage. If you're petite and have a full figure, you probably also have a shorter neck. That extra layer of fabric on your shoulders and arms will cover you up and probably make you look heavy.

There are times when a bride's arms look better covered or maybe she feels more comfortable with a sleeve. Maybe you need a sleeve for religious reasons. If you're going to wear a sleeve, then I recommend choosing one made of a sheer fabric or lace. This will give you coverage yet still look light. If you want the movement of your arms to be less restricted, consider having your seamstress make a bolero, jacket, or shrug. Remember, a set-in sleeve can be very restrictive in a fitted gown. Wearing a veil can also help cover and soften the upper part of the arms. This can provide a small amount of sheer coverage. If you decide to go sleeveless *and* strapless, your bare arms, shoulders, and neck will appear to blend together, making them less noticeable instead of standing out.

BUST

Oh, a woman's bust...the great debate! Some brides want to hide their cleavage. Some want to show it off. Most fiancés want to see it. Of course this is when I remind them, "That's what the honeymoon is for!"

If you are thinking about showing a lot of cleavage, you should really consider the people who will be attending your wedding. Will some of your guests feel uncomfortable seeing too much? If you want to show a bit more cleavage and it doesn't interfere with any religious requirements, I suggest you do it tastefully. Ask yourself this question: "What is the first thing I want everyone to see?" I think the focus should be on *your* beauty, not the girls spilling out the top of your gown!

Because your bust is near your face, it should be taken into consideration when you choose your neckline. Your bust and hips should also be relatively equal in proportion to each other. Here are my suggestions to achieve balance between bust and hips:

SMALL

- Sweetheart necklines can help to add curves.
- Try a gown with ruching or embellishments across your bust.
- Crumb-catchers (vertical pleating or ruching at the bustline) will add fullness to a small bust.
- Padded bra cups can be added to most gowns during alterations, giving your bustline more fullness and a bit of a lift.
- You can wear a plunging or V-neckline.
- Try wearing a halter.
- "Bikini tops" are a fashion-forward option for a woman with a small bust.
- Try an empire waist to accentuate and define your bust.

LARGE

- Adding a slight dip to the neckline of your gown is a minor adjustment that can usually be made in alterations and will soften your bustline.
- An A-line or fuller skirt can balance out a larger bust.
- Try a tip-of-the-shoulder neckline, which will come up higher and give you a bit more coverage than a V-neckline.
- Wearing a tank style or a gown with straps will give you a place to conceal your bra straps if you need that extra support.
- V-necklines can often show too much cleavage.
- A strapless dress with a neckline that goes straight across can make your bust look bigger and shoulders appear broader.
- Avoid halter tops.
- Deep sweetheart necklines may make your bust look too round and show too much cleavage.
- Be careful when wearing a sheath, as it can make you look top-heavy.

WAIST

What woman doesn't want to have a tiny waist? As a general rule, you want your waist to be the smallest part of your torso. Here are some ways to achieve an appealing waist:

SHORT-WAIST

Try wearing a gown with a natural waistline.

LONG-WAIST

Go for a dropped waist. (You may need to have your seamstress alter it to fit lower at your waist.)

SMALL

- You're lucky! You can wear just about anything: natural waist, dropped waist, even an empire.

- Try adding a beaded belt or sash to accentuate your tiny waist.

AVERAGE

Again, you can wear almost any gown style. Look for a dress that balances your bust, waist, and hips.

THICK

- Ruching or pleating, especially on the diagonal, can be very forgiving if you have a fuller midsection or tummy you'd like to camouflage. (Ruching is the irregular gathering or shirring of fabric. Pleating refers to uniform folds in a fabric.)

- A tip-of-the-shoulder gown with full A-line skirt can be one of the best options to minimize your waist. It makes your shoulders look wider and hips appear fuller, making your waist look smaller.

- Sometimes adding a sash or a beaded belt to a gown can make your waist appear smaller.

- Try on a gown with a corset or lace-up back. It can be pulled tightly and give you more shape at your waist. Most gowns follow the natural curves of your body, but a corset can actually change the shape of your body.

- Avoid straight gowns. You want your gown to give you curves, not make you look straight.

The ruching and corset back on Jessica's gown flatter her waist beautifully.

HIPS

Curves are beautiful, but you want your hips to look like they are in proportion to your bust. Here is some advice to make sure your hips look balanced with the rest of your body:

FULL

- An A-line or ball gown skirt may help camouflage full hips.

- A fit-to-flare gown that flares out at the smallest part of your hip will give you a nice shape.

- Tip-of-the-shoulder necklines or cap sleeves can make the shoulders appear wider and balance out your full hips.

- A gown with a natural waist and fuller skirt can sometimes help conceal fuller hips.

- Avoid horizontal seams that fall at the widest point of your hips.

- Avoid bulky skirts with too much gathering.

- Be careful of gowns with too much petticoat in them, which will only add fullness. (Keep in mind, however, that these layers of crinoline or petticoat can be easily removed in alterations and help slim a fuller skirt.)

- Avoid mermaid silhouettes if you have very full hips.

AVERAGE

As long as your hips are in proportion to your bust and waist, you can wear most silhouettes.

SLIM

- Try wearing an A-line or ball gown with a larger skirt to add fullness.

- A gown with a horizontal seam or detail, such as beading, at the low hip can create width.

- Adding a belt or sash can accentuate and define your waist, making your hips appear fuller.

- Sheaths can draw attention to your narrow hips.

This slim A-line gown hugs Jessica's hips perfectly!

HEIGHT

If you are tall and slim, you're lucky and can wear almost any kind of dress.

There's often a bit of confusion with the word *petite*. The term usually refers to a woman's height. Sometimes people use the word to refer to a slim girl because her features are petite. I use the term *petite* in reference to a woman's height. If you are five-foot-four or shorter, then I consider you petite. Petite girls who are thin are also different from petite girls with more curvaceous figures. The same rules don't always apply. Some suggestions for the petite bride:

PETITE FIGURE

- If you are petite and have a small frame, please don't let any dress overpower you. This is really important! Too much dress will only detract from your beauty! This goes for accessories, too. (More on accessories in chapter 7.)

- Look for lighter fabrics, more delicate embellishments, finer laces, and slimmer silhouettes.

- If you have delicate features and want to wear lace, consider a light Chantilly lace, or an Alençon lace with a smaller pattern.

- An empire waist can make you appear taller.

- A natural waist will also make your legs look longer and make you appear taller.

- Princess seams with no waist will give you a clean vertical line and visually add height.

- You can still wear a ball gown, but it would need to be a slimmer style.

- Avoid gowns with a dropped waist that falls very low. This will usually cut you in half.

- If you are petite or have delicate features, avoid large, clunky embellishments like large bows, huge crystals, or overpowering details.

- Avoid really heavy fabrics or heavy guipure laces with large designs.

- Avoid dresses with too many horizontal seams that will visually break up your body.

- If you are very petite, you should avoid silhouettes like mermaid or trumpet with really full bottoms that flare out below the knee. Trust me! You won't be able to walk in a gown that flares out below the knee. Only consider this silhouette if the designer will do a custom measurement, or a "hollow-to-hem," to make the gown in proportion to your height. (More on hollow-to-hem in the appointment chapter, page 145.)

THE PETITE BRIDE

Because Alisa is petite and has a small build, she had to be careful when selecting a wedding gown that was a perfect fit for her body.

She had to make sure the gown didn't overpower her delicate frame. She chose this Reem Acra gown made of soft, light tulle. The grosgrain ribbon at the natural waist gives her a nice proportion. Visually, it makes her legs look longer and gives her the appearance of height. Ladies, if you are petite, you must look at the proportion of your gown carefully! It's easy to find yourself looking for a grand dress and end up with a gown that simply is too much for you.

"BUT RANDY, I'M GOING TO LOSE WEIGHT!"

If you want to lose weight or get in shape for a wedding day, great. I say go for it! But try not to purchase a dress that anticipates a different size than the one you are right now.

Don't forget that your wonderful fiancé fell in love with you as you are, not as you will be after a weight-loss program. There's no reason to add more stress by starving yourself to become an unrealistic size. Personally I don't believe in starving oneself to fit into a dress. You should always be healthy and eat healthy. Love yourself and how you look!

If you are expecting a significant weight loss, ask your consultant about ordering your dress closer to your wedding date. For example, see if you can order your gown four to six months before the wedding rather than the usual eight to twelve months.

PLUS-SIZE

Just because you're plus-size doesn't mean you can't have a great figure! In bridal gowns, *plus-size* is a very subjective term. A plus-size woman can range from someone who doesn't fit into a sample size to a woman who has a *very* full figure. She can be either tall or petite. A plus-size girl may or may not have a really large bust, a fuller waist, or fuller hips. Everyone is different, and you simply cannot lump everyone together in the same category, giving them all one set of rules to follow. I've met girls who are plus-size and *love* their curves! Then I've met curvaceous girls who just want to hide under a big dress. I enjoy working with fuller-figured brides. Unfortunately, full-figured brides have fewer dresses to choose from. Still, they are usually more appreciative when I do find them a gown that flatters them and they realize just how beautiful they truly are. *Everyone* has the right to feel beautiful!

These are some general guidelines plus-size girls may find helpful:

FULLER FIGURE

- Try wearing lighter fabrics that don't look heavy on you.
- A-lines look great on most full-figured women.
- Consider larger embellishments and patterns that may be a better proportion for your body.
- Try bolder, chunkier accessories that are in proportion to your body.

- Avoid dainty accessories that may get lost on you.
- If your bust, waist, and hips are all in proportion, go ahead and try on that gown that hugs your curves.
- A corset or lace-up gown can really mold your shape and give you curves.
- Asymmetrical ruching can be very flattering.

- Avoid slinky fabrics like charmeuse if you need extra support.
- Be careful choosing a gown with an allover sequined or beaded pattern. It may look too flashy and overpowering.
- Look at the back of your gown in the mirror. Make sure you're not spilling over the top.

The list of body combinations and body solutions could go on for pages! However, I have one rule that I feel must always be applied. Whether you're choosing your gown, your accessories, or even your bouquet, you must always look at the silhouette and proportion of everything in relationship to your body! I simply cannot stress this point enough!

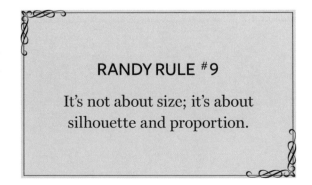

RANDY RULE #9

It's not about size; it's about silhouette and proportion.

No matter what shape or size you are, the right gown can make any woman more beautiful.

SILHOUETTE

You really need to step back and take a good look in the mirror at your silhouette. Does your gown give you a nice, balanced silhouette? Do you look top-heavy? Does your gown make your hips look wide? Do you have a nice defined waist? Again, ideally you want your bust, waist, and hips to have feminine curves that are balanced and create an hourglass shape.

PROPORTION

A good proportion is achieved by the harmonious symmetry and balance of one part of your body in relationship to another part. The parts of your wedding gown and accessories must work in proportion to one another and to your body. Be mindful of where a gown hits your key body parts and divides your body. For a wedding gown to have a successful proportion, the bodice should be one-third or less of your gown's length; the skirt should be two-thirds or more. You can also have the torso be two thirds of the length of your gown with the skirt at one-third. What you want to avoid is a gown that visually cuts your body in half or into three or more sections.

When considering proportion, ask yourself: Is your dress overpowering you? Are your earrings too large for your small face, or so small they get lost? Is your headpiece huge and sitting on top of your head like a punch bowl? Is your bouquet half the size of your body and hiding the entire front of your gown? Is everything balanced? Does anything glaringly stand out? Again, you must look at your entire ensemble to make sure everything is balanced in proportion!

Exceptions to the Rules!

Okay, I've just given you all the rules for what you should wear for your body. If you follow these guidelines, you should have some success in finding your perfect dress. However, you must again remember that these are just guidelines!

For every rule I have given you, trust me, I can show you a gown that breaks it. This is why I said this is a trick question. I tell you not to wear ruching across the bust if your bust is fuller. I can show you a dress that looks great on a full-busted girl that will break this rule. I also say don't wear a sweetheart neckline if you have a full bust, yet I have a gown with a sweetheart neckline that accommodates a full bust beautifully! This is why you absolutely must try a gown on to see how it fits your body!

To illustrate this point, I'm going to give you a specific example of an exception to my rules. I suggest that if you are petite in height and full-figured, you should avoid wearing horizontal bands and heavy re-embroidered lace. After my "Randy's Recap" is the story of a time when I broke this rule— and it worked out beautifully for my bride Jessica.

Randy's Recap

EVERY DRESS IS CUT DIFFERENTLY

•

DON'T LET ANYONE PUT YOU IN A BOX OR COMPARE YOU TO A FRUIT

•

TRY TO CHOOSE A GOWN WITH THE CORRECT PROPORTIONS

•

SMALLER FRAMES TEND TO LOOK BETTER WITH LIGHTER FABRICS
AND MORE DELICATE DETAILS

•

LARGER FRAMES CAN WEAR LARGER, BOLDER EMBELLISHMENTS,
DETAILS, AND ACCESSORIES

•

SILHOUETTE AND PROPORTION ARE TWO OF THE MOST IMPORTANT
THINGS TO REMEMBER WHEN CHOOSING A WEDDING DRESS

•

EVERY BODY IS SHAPED DIFFERENTLY

JESSICA AND MATT'S $\mathcal{S}$TORY

Hometown	Houston, Texas
Wedding Date	June 19
Location	Westminster United Methodist Church, Houston, Texas
Wedding Guests	150
Dress Designer	Rivini

Jessica and her mother agree on one point: Finding a wedding dress for a full-figured woman can be a nightmare. Jessica and her mother visited several bridal boutiques in Texas where the consultants held gowns in front of her body and she was asked to "imagine" what the dresses would look like in her size. Spending that much money to use their imaginations seemed like an awful lot to ask!

I first saw Jessica when her wedding planner e-mailed me a photo of her and her fiancé. Her planner told me she liked lace and wanted a dress that had a traditional, yet modern feel. I actually picked out a gown for Jessica before I even met her. When I met Jessica and her family in person, I remember thinking just how beautiful she was and what a caring and close-knit family she had. The first gown Jessica tried on was the one that I had chosen for her. She loved it! We were both concerned, however, that the only reason she loved it so much was because this was the first gown in her size—the first gown she had even been able to try on her body. To make sure the gown was the one, she spent three more hours trying on thirty more dresses. She ended up with the original gown I had chosen for her.

What's surprising is that this dress features elements that I would normally tell a woman who is petite and has a fuller figure not to wear. It has five tiers of horizontal lace running across the body, which can make a woman appear shorter and wider. But this gown looks beautiful on Jessica!

The gown had a small band of beading under the bust that we replaced with a larger jeweled band that was a better proportion for Jessica. The final touch to Jessica's gown was a piece of lace from her mother's wedding dress, which she had sewn into the lining.

"That moment—walking down the aisle arm in arm with my dad—was unlike any other. I know the dress made a difference. I felt perfect. After everything that had happened, I got everything I ever wanted—and more. I thank Randy for a lot of that."

You can tell Jessica looks and feels gorgeous!

CHAPTER FIVE

YOUR *LOOK*

The look of your wedding dress is directly related to your theme

Deciding on what your look will be for your wedding day is one of the most important steps you will take in helping you find your perfect dress. How can you possibly choose a dress for your big day if you're not clear about how you want to look? When I meet with brides, one of the first questions I ask them is: "How do you want to *look* on your wedding day?" Most brides have one very similar answer. None of them wants to be a typical bride. It seems that each woman is looking for that special *something* to set her wedding apart

from all the ones she's seen. Every bride is looking to make some kind of unique, personal statement. These different aspirations are what make my job interesting and fun!

So what is your "look" and how do you find it? And how do you communicate it to your consultant? In this chapter, I will help you find your look by showing you looks from other brides I have worked with. Each bride's look is a personal expression of her style, taste, vision, and imagination. Hopefully, seeing these brides' wedding looks will inspire you, and help you to define yours. I will also help you find the words to clearly communicate your look to your consultant. This is very important. If you are not able to share your vision with your consultant, finding your dress will certainly be more difficult.

The look of your wedding dress is directly related to your theme. The look of your wedding should be consistent in everything from your wedding dress (of course) to your groom's clothes, your invitations, flowers, music, food, and all the other details of the day.

Perhaps the best way for me to explain a bride's look is to show you. I selected nine brides from my book's photo shoot who each created a look that worked perfectly for her story—and for her big day.

Your look...

- Can tell the *story* of you and your fiancé.

- Is influenced by the budget, location, season, time, and timeline you chose in your *plan*.

- Is enhanced by elements in the design of the *gown*.

- Should flatter your *body*.

The look of your wedding should be consistent in everything from your wedding dress (of course) to your groom's clothes, your invitations, flowers, music, food, and all the other details of the day.

Princess

For many, the term *princess* is synonymous with weddings. For decades girls have dreamed of fairy-tale stories complete with a prince, a castle, and someday becoming a princess. A gown for a traditional princess look usually has a full ball gown skirt with a very long train and lots of beading, lace, and crystals. Think of Princess Grace or Princess Diana.

Of course, our most recent princess bride, Catherine Middleton, chose the perfect look for her wedding to Prince William. Her dress had a ball gown silhouette with exquisite custom lace and a flawless fit, which made quite a regal statement and perfectly reflected her personality—timeless and understated—yet had a grand train. Her tiara, earrings, bouquet, and train were all in perfect proportion. I think it will go down in history as one of the best wedding ensembles of all time!

What differentiates a modern princess from a traditional one? Typically it means a current interpretation of the traditional princess gown's silhouette, the fabric, and embellishments. Your accessories can definitely help to create and define it. This bride will choose to wear a jeweled head-band or crystal pins in her hair instead of the usual tiara or crown. Here is an example of a modern princess.

ANNA LISA AND GEOFFREY

Hometown: Westchester, NY; *Wedding Date:* May 8; *Location:* Glen Island Harbour, New Rochelle, NY; *Wedding Guests:* 220; *Dress Designer:* Monique Lhuillier

For Anna, the transformation into a modern princess came easy since she is an assistant to the president of a jewelry manufacturer. Because Anna knew a little something about sparkle, when it came time for her to select a dress for her fairy-tale wedding, she was drawn to one that looked like a piece of jewelry. The Monique Lhuillier gown had a silk satin-organza A-line skirt and a jewel-encrusted bodice.

When Anna purchased her dress, there was just one catch to her fairy-tale story: She wasn't exactly engaged yet to her boyfriend, Geoffrey. But the moment Anna saw the dress, she knew she'd found her Cinderella gown. Beginning with her first glance at this dress, it was clear that her wedding would center on sparkle and the bold, bright, and daring princess Anna knew she could be. So even without an engagement ring on her finger Anna went ahead and bought the jeweled dress she loved.

Anna confessed to Geoffrey about purchasing the dress, and a magical three months later he proposed. One year later, they were officially united.

Anna knows that her dress set the tone for her modern princess look and everything that transpired on her big day.

Anna's modern princess gown.

Fantasy

The concept of "fantasy" plays into our imagination and desire to bring dream-like images and elements to life. This bride wants her wedding to be a magical celebration that takes her away from everyday reality. Her story is one that uses words like: *magical*, *dramatic*, *avant-garde*, *theatrical*, *artistic*, and *creative*. In the world of bridal gowns, this can be realized with gowns that are ethereal, over-the-top creations. In the case of Jessica and Nelson, their idea of a fantasy wedding took flight!

JESSICA AND NELSON

Hometown: Mamaroneck, NY; *Wedding Date:* May 30; *Location:* Lyndhurst Castle, Tarrytown, NY; *Wedding Guests:* 185; *Dress Designer:* Pnina Tornai

Jessica and Nelson's relationship was written in the stars! They met and fell in love while working at Archie comics, where they shared a love of fantasy, filled with imagination. When it came time to plan their wedding, Jessica knew exactly the look she wanted for their day: a fairy-tale wedding complete with a gown that had real *wings*. Yes, wings! In contrast with the traditional and modern princesses, Jessica was a surreal twenty-first-century fairy-tale princess.

When I met Jessica, she told me she wanted a gown that looked like a fairy princess by artist Amy Brown. She then told me she was going to wear wings with her gown. This was definitely one of the most unusual requests I had ever had. I immediately went to my computer and did a search for Amy Brown's work. Once I saw her beautiful illustrations online and Jessica told me her vision, I knew exactly which gown to pull for her!

A magical crystal-studded lace-and-tulle gown by Pnina Tornai with a corset bodice was perfect for her desired fantasy look. After the dress was ordered, Jessica found someone to create her fairy wings. They were magnificent!

"I had long extensions put into my hair and I wore a jeweled headband and real flowers with crystals in the center," Jessica said. Walking up the aisle at Lyndhurst Castle in Tarrytown, New York, with her dad dressed as a wizard, toward her fiancé dressed in the armor of Portugal's first king—and with many of the guests in costume, too—Jessica's childhood fantasy came true.

With her fairy wings, Jessica got the fantasy look she dreamed of.

Romantic

A romantic look is soft, feminine, and ethereal. A romantic wedding gown features delicate fabrics like lace, organza, and tulle, and embellishments such as flowers and bows. It has softer, more feminine detailing and uses more tonal beading in place of larger rhinestones. The silhouette is often softer and more fluid than a structured gown. Words like *soft*, *feminine*, *flowy*, *billowy*, *lacy*, *fluid*, and *frothy* are perfect for describing a romantic look.

ALLISON AND TOM

Hometown: Stony Brook, NY; *Wedding Date:* July 10; *Location:* Ali's Family Home, Stony Brook, NY; *Wedding Guests:* 200; *Dress Designer:* Christos

Allison was blessed to have four sets of grandparents attend her wedding. Her day was all about family, and the look of the day complemented the love and romance that was all around. Ever since Allison was a little girl, she'd read bridal magazines, dreaming of her day. She knew what she didn't want: a fancy, indoor, formal, ballroom wedding. What she did want: an outdoor, garden, romantic wedding. She wanted the wedding to look and feel like home.

Allison was clear about her wedding look but she was torn between two dresses and asked me to break the tie for her. She looked so gorgeous and fresh in the Christos dress with the dotted tulle and the flowers on the waistband. The gown was soft, feminine, and organic looking. It epitomized all the design elements she was seeking in her dress and was the perfect look for her romantic, outdoor wedding.

Ultimately, Allison chose the Christos gown, and it became the inspiration for all the other elements at the wedding: birchwood signs, burlap, lavender, and other rustic yet elegant accents. Since her husband-to-be was not a formal kind of guy, the laid-back "home" wedding look was especially nice: Tom wore tailored linen khaki pants.

And so it was: a relaxed wedding on the lawn of the house where she'd lived all her life, surrounded by family and loved ones…how romantic!

Allison chose soft layers of dotted tulle and a rose at the waist to achieve her romantic look.

Vintage

Brides often tell me they want to borrow elements from the past for a vintage-inspired look for their wedding. Whether you decide to wear your mother's wedding gown, find a gown from a vintage shop, or purchase a new gown and add your own heirloom jewelry and accessories, there are numerous ways (and many fashionable periods of time to choose from) to achieve a vintage look for your wedding day.

You may want to wear a gown draped in chiffon that has a Grecian feeling or a regal ball gown that has elements taken from the Elizabethan or Victorian era. Maybe you have a love affair with the Roaring Twenties and decide to wear a flapper-inspired look that is fun and flirty, or choose a sleek glamorous look inspired by the Hollywood screen goddesses from the 1930s and '40s. You may desire that classic Audrey Hepburn or Grace Kelly look taken right out of the pages of *Vogue* from the 1950s, or a short and sassy style from the 1960s. No matter what period of fashion you borrow from, choosing a look that celebrates and embraces the fashion from the past while incorporating your own style can be a fantastic way to create a totally fresh and timeless look for your big day.

Here are three of my brides who were inspired by fashion from the past and used this inspiration to create their own look for their wedding.

Vintage 1920s
KATE AND GLEB

Hometown: Brooklyn, NY; *Wedding Date:* October 10; *Location:* Lyndhurst Castle, Tarrytown, NY; *Wedding Guests:* 135; *Dress Designer:* Claire Pettibone

Kate knew from the very beginning that she wanted a dress by Claire Pettibone. Claire is a designer known for her soft-bodied dresses that have an ethereal and somewhat bohemian style. Kate felt that the dress she chose was the perfect reflection of her and Gleb's own real-life story. It was bohemian all the way with just a hint of the 1920s. Born in different parts of Russia, Kate and Gleb moved to the United States, where they met each other.

Kate and Gleb were married at a castle in a ceremony that was a collage of various styles, directed by their interfaith minister. In fact, their entire wedding paid homage to different religions, cultures, and traditions, and celebrated different periods throughout time.

From Japanese lucky charms passed to guests, to a flower girl carrying enormous felt flowers down the aisle, to a Tibetan bowl ceremony with its powerful circle of silence, each part of the wedding was filled with meaning. And Kate's dress

Kate in her 1920s-inspired gown.

fit in perfectly with her bohemian style. She wore her hair in finger waves and added a long strand of pearls around her neck to complete her 1920s look.

For the reception, Kate's musical family—brother, mother, father—played an inspired set of jazz and 1920s songs for the crowd. Kate and Gleb's friend actually choreographed their dance. And the best part about their dance: the way Kate's dress moved on the floor! For this couple, it was all about the dress.

Vintage 1930s–1940s
BREANNE AND TREVOR

Hometown: Manhattan, NY; *Wedding Date:* October 30; *Location:* The Breakers, Palm Beach, FL; *Wedding Guests:* 150; *Dress Designer:* Carolina Herrera

"My wedding was a party more than anything else," Breanne said, describing her special destination wedding in Palm Beach, Florida. Breanne and her "Irish boy from Dublin" fiancé, Trevor, wanted a wedding where their guests were able to get away from daily life and have a vacation to remember. Breanne chose a Carolina Herrera dress, inspired by a painting by John Singer Sargent, which reflected the chic, bold, and dramatic elements of her and Trevor's big weekend event.

The dress itself was unlike anything Breanne had ever worn before. It was dramatic with an asymmetrical draped front panel and long slit up the front.

The gown is made of a silk faille, and is quite chic and modern; yet because of its silhouette, it looks like it descended from the late 1930s or early 1940s. The two beaded "brooches" on the bodice, the peep-toe Christian Louboutin shoes Breanne wore, and the cage veil perched atop her 1930s hairstyle emphasized her retro look.

Breanne chose a cage veil and peep-toe shoes for her retro look.

Vintage 1950s
JENNIFER AND JARRET

Hometown: Sheffield, PA, for her; Seattle, WA, for him; *Wedding Date:* September 18; *Location:* Boathouse in Prospect Park, Brooklyn, NY; *Wedding Guests:* 85; *Dress Designer:* Rivini

The 1950s are absolutely my favorite decade for fashion! Christian Dior launched his "New Look" in 1947, and his wasp-waisted designs and voluminous skirts instantly became the fashion standard. With its strapless bodice, natural waist, and very full A-line skirt, Jennifer's gown, designed by Rivini, looks like it stepped out of the 1950s. It's made of a sheer, silk organza, and has delicate three-dimensional roses sewn onto the skirt. Jennifer's upswept hairstyle, reminiscent of the 1950s beehive, completed her retro-inspired look.

When Jennifer and Jarret auditioned bands for their wedding, they would ask them to play "The Way You Look Tonight." The only thing Jennifer knew for sure was that she wanted a wedding gown that looked like a dress Audrey Hepburn would have worn in the 1954 movie *Sabrina*. "I remember when I tried the dress on for the first time," said Jennifer. "'The Way You Look Tonight' was playing throughout the salon. The song became such an important part of our wedding-planning process that Jarret and I even chose it for our first dance at our reception! My mom told me that she wanted me to get a dress that made me emotional and not to get a dress because it was the right price. I actually bought two dresses: one for the ceremony and one for the cake cutting. But I loved my first dress so much that I didn't even change gowns. Randy gave me the confidence to make fashion decisions. He made me realize that I could put on a dress and feel like a million dollars. I know I love this dress. More important, it loves me back."

Jennifer's hair, strapless bodice, natural waist, and full skirt were perfect for her 1950s look.

Understated

When you ask me which dress style I recommend most for brides, it's one of understated elegance. Words like *simple, clean, understated, classic, timeless, unfussy,* and *minimalist* are perfect to describe this look. I love a clean, understated look and believe a gown should enhance a woman's beauty and not take away from or overpower her. An understated wedding gown allows the bride to add her own jewelry and accessories for extra drama. By the time a bride adds a headpiece, veil, earrings, bracelet, shoes, and bouquet, she can end up getting lost. Taking a luxurious fabric, manipulating it to create a beautiful silhouette, and adding touches of exquisite detailing to a gown can be stunning!

JILL AND MATTHEW

Hometown: Pembroke Pines, FL, and Livingston, NJ; *Wedding Date:* March 6; *Location:* Delray Beach, FL; *Wedding Guests:* 200; *Dress Designer:* Romona Keveza

Jill's gown designed by Romona Keveza is a perfect example of understated elegance. Sumptuous silk taffeta has been carefully draped to create the ruched sweetheart bodice and simple fit-to-flare skirt. When the consultant asked Jill how she wanted to look, she quickly replied, "I want a look that reflects my personal style on my wedding day: simple and classic. I never cried or got that 'aha moment,' but as soon as I slipped this dress on my sister told me she had no doubt it was my dress. I tried on several other dresses, but couldn't get this one out of my head."

Jill and Matthew took photos before the wedding, and Jill remembered when they saw each other for the first time. "It was incredible! To share that special moment with our closest family and friends made us so happy. I remember we both actually began to laugh." Jill personalized her look by adding an exquisite brooch by Thomas Knoell at the natural waist. For the photo shoot, we styled Jill's hair up and gave her a glorious triple-layer organza coat, also by Romona Keveza, that added lots of drama to her understated, elegant look.

Jill went clean, simple, and understated. We added the organza coat for a bit of drama.

Glamorous

Fashionable, chic, dramatic, stylish, and *sexy* are just a few words that can be used to describe a glamorous look. The term *glamorous* conjures up thoughts of Hollywood's screen goddesses. Think of actresses like Rita Hayworth, Susan Hayward, Marlene Dietrich, Kate Winslet, Penélope Cruz, Scarlett Johansson, and Nicole Kidman. A bride who wants a glamorous look definitely wants to make a spectacular statement when she walks down the aisle. Dramatic or extravagant makeup, hair, veil, or accessories can heighten a glamorous look.

ALEXIS AND JOEY

Hometown: New York, NY; *Wedding Date:* February 27; *Location:* Viscaya Museum and Gardens, Miami, FL; *Wedding Guests:* 200; *Dress Designer:* Pnina Tornai

This New York native knew exactly what wedding look she wanted: old Hollywood glamour all the way! Alexis found the ideal dress that made her feel like Ginger Rogers. As soon as she put the dress on, Alexis knew it was right. In the changing room and throughout the salon, she occasionally twirled around to watch the skirt glisten under the lights. The lace gown had a full A-line skirt and was covered with sparkling sequins. A strap on one shoulder and the hemline were both covered with tufts of beaded lace that looked like feathers. A headpiece of feathers added even more glamour to her look.

For the wedding, she and her fiancé, Joey, decided to plan a glamorous party in Miami, and Alexis's dress set the tone for everything. Everything, that is, except for the massive monsoon that hit Florida, and the massive snowstorm in New York, where most of her family was traveling from. Many of the wedding guests were stranded in airports or hotels for up to twenty-seven hours. Thirty people had to cancel. Even Alexis's makeup artist couldn't get a flight, but luckily made it at 2 AM the night before the wedding.

On the morning of her wedding, Alexis had to dig deep to compensate for all the things around her that seemed to be going wrong. The whole wedding was supposed to take place outside, so the pictures were ruined by the rain. What was she supposed to do? What made her feel better? The dress, of course! Once she slipped it on, something incredible happened. As the ceremony began, the rain stopped, the sun came out, and a double rainbow graced the skies. Alexis threw her shoulders back and let the dress be her guide that evening. As Frank Sinatra played, Alexis and her new husband celebrated their modern-day wedding in old-time style. As they were dancing together, they realized that some old Hollywood magic had taken place, just like in the movies. Now, talk about glamour!

Alexis looking and feeling glamorous!

Nontraditional

Most sources tell us there are a few different types of brides, and then squeeze everyone into a category. I don't believe everyone fits neatly into a category or type. Brides today are multifaceted. If you don't feel like you can be defined by one look, try combining more than one. You can mix and match different components to create something entirely new that's personal to you.

For example, I worked with a bride once who had a Gothic look. Her hair was dyed jet black, and she had several piercings and tattoos. To my surprise, my Goth bride wanted a fairly traditional wedding! To celebrate both sides of her personality, I picked out a traditional wedding dress with lace, as she wanted, but then suggested she accentuate that dress with a black sash to reflect the more unique side of her personality. She didn't realize that she could incorporate traditional and Goth together. And PS she looked amazing!

Many also tell you that if you have any tattoos, you should try to cover them up on your wedding day. I disagree. When I ask brides why they got their tattoos, they tell me because they think they look pretty!

If you have a beautiful tattoo and it's a part of your story, instead of trying to cover it up, you may want to showcase it on your wedding day.

Well, I promised you this wasn't going to be your mother's wedding book.

Today more and more brides are discovering that they don't fit into a prescribed category. Every person in the world is different and has a unique story to tell. Every day I work with mature brides who are getting married later in life or for the second time. I meet expectant brides. I also have brides who are having same sex weddings. The same rules apply for these brides: They should still follow my five essentials. Find your story and make your plan. Learn about gowns and your body, and discover your look.

SEXY

"I want to look sexy" are words I hear quite often from brides searching for their gown! However, *sexy* is a very relative term. And a sexy gown doesn't necessarily mean risqué. A bride can wear a high-neck, long-sleeved, floor-length gown and still look sexy. An hourglass silhouette, a woman's bare shoulders, or a graceful collarbone can all be sexy. A gown with a low back or sheer midriff can be sexy. The way a gown drapes across your body or highlights your curves can make it sexy. For me, sexy means that someone is attracted to the way you look. And who in the world doesn't want that? When speaking with your consultant, be sure to elaborate the specific details you desire for your gown to be sexy.

Instead of covering them up, why not show off your beautiful tattoos?

DESCRIBING YOUR LOOK

One of the most difficult things for some brides is finding the perfect words to describe their look. Even brides who may have decided on their look may still not be able to articulate it. When I ask, "How do you want to look on your wedding day?" some brides will gaze at me with a blank stare, completely at a loss for the best words to use.

Hopefully you've thought about your look while reading this chapter. To make it easier for you to convey your vision, here are some words that you can use to describe your look to your consultant. **Feel free to mix and match these words to create the most descriptive explanation.**

AGE-APPROPRIATE	EXOTIC	MAGICAL	SEDUCTIVE
ANGELIC	FANTASY	MAJESTIC	SEXY
ARCHITECTURAL	FASHION-FORWARD	MINIMAL	SHOWY
AVANT-GARDE	FEMININE	MODERN	SIMPLE
BOHEMIAN	FLASHY	MODEST	SLEEK
BOLD	FLIRTY	NONTRADITIONAL	SOFT
CHIC	FLOWY	OPULENT	SOPHISTICATED
CLASSIC	FORMAL	ORGANIC	SPARKLING
CLASSY	FORMFITTING	ORNATE	STATUESQUE
CLEAN	FRESH	OVER-THE-TOP	STRIKING
COMFORTABLE	FUN	POOFY	SUBTLE
CONSERVATIVE	FUNKY	PRINCESS	SWEET
CONTEMPORARY	GLAMOROUS	PROVOCATIVE	TAILORED
CURVACEOUS	GLITZY	QUIRKY	TIMELESS
CUTTING-EDGE	GODDESS	REFINED	TRADITIONAL
DARING	GOTHIC	REGAL	TRENDY
DAZZLING	GRAND	RELAXED	UNCONVENTIONAL
DELICATE	GRECIAN	RESERVED	UNDERSTATED
DRAMATIC	INFORMAL	RETRO	UNEXPECTED
EDGY	INNOCENT	ROMANTIC	UNFUSSY
ELEGANT	LACY	ROYAL	VINTAGE
EMBELLISHED	LIGHT	RUFFLED	VOLUPTUOUS
ETHEREAL	LUXURIOUS	SASSY	WHIMSICAL

Randy's Recap

YOUR STORY, PLAN, BODY, THE STYLE OF GOWN YOU WANT,
AND ACCESSORIES ARE COMBINED TO CREATE
YOUR WEDDING "LOOK"

•

THERE ARE MANY WAYS TO INTERPRET YOUR LOOK,
AND THE DETAILS MAY BE PERSONAL AND UNIQUE

•

USE A FEW DESCRIPTIVE WORDS TO CLEARLY
COMMUNICATE YOUR LOOK TO YOUR CONSULTANT

•

YOUR LOOK SHOULD BE CONSISTENT WITH
THE THEME OF YOUR WEDDING

•

THERE IS NO SUCH THING AS A "TYPICAL" BRIDE

•

TRY COMBINING SEVERAL COMPONENTS
TO CREATE YOUR OWN LOOK

•

NOT EVERYONE FITS INTO A CATEGORY

•

EMBRACE YOUR PERSONAL BEAUTY, STORY, AND STYLE!

LINDA AND MITCH'S *Story*

Hometown	Rye, New York, for her and Trumbull, Connecticut, for him
Wedding Date	October 2
Location	Rye Presbyterian Church
Wedding Guests	186
Dress Designer	Elizabeth Fillmore

Linda met her husband on Match.com. She's sixty-two. He's seventy-five. She called Mitch "a heart walking around on two legs." Before they met, they had both been married to other partners for many years and were widowed.

"At our age, our lives are like four funerals and a wedding!" Linda jokes. "Mitch and I decided we could either have big lavish funerals when we passed, or celebrate our love with a wedding that we could enjoy together."

Linda credited her nephew Freddy and her son, William, with getting her out of her own way to try new things. "My children are my heroes," she said. "William and Amy got me to see the next chapter.

"I wasn't quite sure how to do it," Linda revealed, referring to her impending wedding. She did get herself to a salon in the city to look at wedding dresses. Elizabeth Fillmore was doing a trunk show at the salon, and she personally fitted the dress for Linda. She said she'd make whatever adjustments Linda needed: a little more fabric on the sleeve, and that was about it.

When I saw Linda in the dress, which was floor-length, I knew something else was missing. She needed a veil to complete her look and make her really feel like a bride.

She thought differently, however. "For me to go down the aisle in church wearing a cathedral-length veil and a long white dress, I felt like I was giving everyone permission to laugh at me. But really I had to give myself permission to seize the moment!"

This wedding—and by association, this dress—were part of the same thing: a chance to express gratitude. Linda was deeply grateful for all those years people were supportive to her and her children before and after her husband passed away. The wedding was a thank-you to them for their steadfastness, a celebration for everyone. "What I felt strongly was that people had supported us. The lace dress I wore was a nod to my own strength, but it was a strength that came from so many others."

Linda is proof that women are beautiful at any age!

CHAPTER SIX

YOUR *APPOINTMENT*

There is a smart way to approach a bridal appointment so that it benefits both bride and consultant to the fullest

This is the chapter you've been waiting for. This is the moment in the process when it all starts to not only come together, but also come to life. You actually get to try on those dresses and put the five essentials into action.

I meet with almost a hundred brides a day. I see them at each stage of the bridal appointment. I watch them enter the salon. I notice whether or not they're prepared, and what their expectations are. I see the meltdowns, the domineering moth-

ers, the tearful fathers, the jealous sisters, and the crazy families. Trust me, I've seen it all.

You want to get as much as possible accomplished in the allotted time without anxiety. Remember, this is a day you should be spending with loved ones and trying on beautiful dresses. This should be *fun*!

My wish is for you to go into your appointment Educated, Elevated, and Empowered!

PREPARING FOR YOUR APPOINTMENT

Gather Photos

I suggest that you browse magazines and websites and tear out or print out photographs of the kinds of dresses you want to wear. I like brides to bring in about five to ten photographs when they come in to shop for a dress. Don't bring in too many. Remember, your bridal appointment is usually an hour and a half.

Once I had a bride who showed up for her appointment with more than eighty photos! Think about it! There is absolutely no way any human being can try on that many dresses during one appointment.

Photos tell a consultant what kind of dress you like. Usually, a consultant can look at those photographs and get a clear sense of your style. I find that brides often choose dresses from the same designer. If you do, there may be a dress from that designer that you've never seen that the consultant can show you. Photos help articulate and express what you're feeling but may have trouble putting into words. They also help tell your story.

NOTICE THE DETAILS ABOUT YOUR PHOTOS: WHAT THINGS DO THESE DRESSES HAVE IN COMMON?

- Are the dresses all the same silhouette?

- Are all the dresses within the budget you've established?

- Are they right for the season and location of your wedding?

- Are they all ornately embellished?

- Are they all the same fabric?

- Are the dresses in the photos telling your story?

A mood board with inspirational photos can help a consultant find your perfect gown.

Select the Right Salon

Avoid unnecessary disappointments on the day of your appointment with detailed preparation. For example, once you have some dresses in mind, you can call your salon *before* you make an appointment to see if the dresses you like are carried in their inventory, and if the dresses are in stock. Of course you want to choose a salon that can offer you a nice selection with many of the designers and dresses you like. Some stores have websites so you can check their inventory, too.

Check the shops that carry dress styles you like and find out about salon hours and prices. The right salon should have almost everything you need, including in-house alterations and dress cleaning and pressing. They should have courteous and knowledgeable consultants, plus a nice selection of accessories and shoes. Does the salon have a large inventory of gowns for *all* body types, including samples in plus sizes if needed?

What to Bring to Your Appointment

Come to a bridal appointment dressed appropriately. Since you will be undressing in front of your consultant, you should wear clothing that you can change into and out of easily. Most important: Remember to wear the proper undergarments. They will probably provide you with a robe and a long-line bra if you need, but you may bring your own if you wish. Avoid wearing black or dark-colored underwear, as it can show through the white dresses and be distracting. Always wear underwear! Salons will not allow you to try on gowns without it.

If you can, wear a pair of shoes with the same heel height you are considering wearing at the wedding. I think it's always good to bring something with a little height, like a pump or heel.

Don't wear clunky accessories to your appointment. You want to eliminate anything that may detract from the dresses you are trying on.

Bring a camera. Most salons do not let you take a photograph until you purchase a dress. But you want to be ready to snap one if you do. You will also want to take pictures of any changes you are making to the gown. (More on that on page 146.)

Who to Bring to Your Appointment

Only invite people who love and support you—and who *understand* your story, your style, your budget, and are there to offer you love and support.

Don't bring anyone who is negative or is not looking out for *your* best interests!

Don't bring along people who upset you or push your buttons.

Try to keep your group small. Things can get confusing with too many people and too many opinions flying around the salon.

Don't bring someone who will take control of your gown appointment.

If someone else is helping pay for your gown, they may want to be there when you choose it. They will probably want to voice their opinion—however, make sure you don't end up with a gown of *their* dreams instead of *yours*!

Should you bring your fiancé? Tradition dictates that a bride keep her gown hidden from her fiancé until the moment she walks down the aisle or until the morning of the wedding. However, some brides choose to have their fiancés there as a part of the selection process. This is up to you. If your fiancé knows your story, your style, and your

KEY QUESTIONS TO ASK WHEN SELECTING A SALON

- What is the price range of the wedding dresses at the salon?

- Which designers does the salon carry?

- Do they carry the designers you are interested in?

- Does the salon carry the sizes that you need?

- Do they have a top-notch alterations department, or will you have to go somewhere else for your alterations?

- How much are alterations, or are they included in the price?

- Does the salon sell accessories?

- Do they have any trunk shows for designers you wish to see?

- Do they have sample sales? (See page 30 for a brief description of sample sales.)

- How long is an appointment at your salon?

- What is their policy if you cancel your appointment?

When selecting a salon for your appointment, make sure the salon is reputable!

The right salon should have almost everything you need, including in-house alterations and dress cleaning and pressing.

Make sure you choose the gown of *your* dreams.

> ## RANDY RULE # 10
>
> Everyone has an opinion.
> Make sure yours is heard.

budget, has good taste in clothes, and you want his opinion, then I say: Bring him!

Make sure that whomever you bring to your appointment is there to help you find *your* dress and not just to voice an opinion about what they like. Sometimes a bride comes in with a huge group of people, and everyone seems to have an opinion. When this happens, it can be difficult for the bride to make a decision.

When I see this happen, I turn to everyone and ask, "What is your favorite flower?"

One person says poppy, while another says hydrangea; someone else says roses or maybe calla lilies. Everyone usually has a different favorite flower. Finally, I turn to the bride and ask her the same question. Inevitably she answers something completely different from the rest of her group. Maybe she says, "I love peonies." At that moment I turn to her and say, "So why would you walk down the aisle as a poppy, a rose, or a hydrangea when you love peonies?"

I ask this question to demonstrate that everyone has a different preference—whether it's in flowers or wedding dresses. You may certainly want to consider other opinions, but I want you to follow *your* preference when it comes to the dress.

THE APPOINTMENT

Check In, and Make Sure You're on Time

You don't want to feel rushed. You want this day to run smoothly. Make sure you've eaten and are well rested—you don't want to make this important decision when you're not thinking clearly.

Meet Your Consultant

She'll greet you and take you back into a fitting room, where you can talk. She will probably explain the "rules of engagement" and let you know if they are featuring a trunk show with a particular designer. This is your chance to talk and ask questions! If you are not prepared, you probably won't have the best experience; in the end, the appointment will most likely be a waste of your and your consultant's time.

Communicate the Five Essentials

This is where details matter: Tell your consultant your story and plan. Discuss the photos you brought. Tell her your budget, the location, and the date of your wedding. You need to paint the whole picture. Always be honest! The only way your consultant can truly help you is if she understands your *real* budget and the other details of your wedding.

After a brief consultation, your consultant will go to the stockroom to pull your first dress choices. She may also want the chance to pull something of her choosing, too. Let her! She may bring in something that you hadn't thought of that could potentially be your dream dress. You should trust the professionals during this process and keep an open mind.

After the consultant leaves the room, you will slip into your bra, shoes, and robe.

When your consultant returns with the dresses, look at them. This is when the fun begins! You should start by trying on the dress you like the most.

TRUNK SHOWS

Often bridal salons have trunk shows to showcase specific designers. The term *trunk show* originated back in the day when designers would ship their dresses cross-country in steamer trunks. A salon usually carries a sampling of a designer's collection, but a trunk show usually includes the *entire* collection of new dresses (some just off the runway that aren't even in stores yet), as well as best sellers from past seasons. This has its advantages and its disadvantages for the bride.

One huge advantage is that if you find you like a particular designer's dresses, a trunk show is an opportunity to see all of their designs on display at one time. Also, during a trunk show there are promotions offered, which could mean you get a good discount on a dress you love. You may also have a chance to work directly with a designer or a representative for that designer to get custom changes to gowns that are not normally available to brides.

However, you must be ready to purchase the dress on the spot in order to get both the discount and the dress. Trunk show promotional discounts are only good *at* the show. And the show will be moving to a new location after it ends, so there is no guarantee you will see that dress again. Your salon may not carry that particular dress or order it for its inventory at a later date.

Pamela knew this lace gown was right for her as soon as she put it on.

Be sure to communicate clearly what you like and dislike about the gown to your consultant. This is *very* important in helping guide her to find your perfect dress! You should be able to do this fairly well with the knowledge you've gained from the previous chapters of this book.

What do you do if you fall in love with the first dress you try on? Should you keep shopping if you know that first gown is "the one"? I would probably try on a couple more just to reinforce the fact that this is *the* gown.

I often have brides who fall in love with the first gown they try on. Actually, I would estimate that about 70 to 80 percent of my brides who end up purchasing, buy one of the first three gowns they try on! Why is this, you may ask? I believe it's because these brides have done their home work. They know their story, their plan, and they know how they want to look on their wedding day. I also believe it happens more often when you have a great consultant who really listens to you and knows how to pull the right dresses.

I recall when a dear friend of mine, Ramona, who was engaged, came in to the salon with a photo of a gown that she pulled out of a magazine. She said it was the only gown she had ever seen that she truly loved. She put the gown on and immediately said, "This is the one!" She wouldn't even try on any other gowns. That's how confident she was that it was the right dress for her. Sometimes you just know it!

But this doesn't always happen. If you don't like the dress, then quickly move on to the next one. Remember, there is a time limit for your appointment. Don't waste your time standing in a gown you don't like. You will run out of time and end up disappointed that you only got to try on a few dresses during your appointment. I say, "If you don't like it, take it off!"

If none of the dresses your consultant has brought in for you work, use the vocabulary I've given you to express to the consultant what you do and do not like about them. When you move to round two of dress selection, the consultant will have an even better idea about what to bring.

Be sure to communicate clearly what you like and dislike about the gown to your consultant. This is *very* important in helping guide her to find your perfect dress!

WHEN YOU STEP INTO THE DRESS, ASK YOURSELF:

- Do I like this gown?

- When I put the dress on, what do I see?

- How does the dress make me feel?

- How does my body look in this gown?

- Does it fit my venue?

- Is it comfortable to wear?

- Am I wearing the gown, or is it overpowering and wearing me?

- Is it the right silhouette?

- Is it the right color?

- Does it come in the color I want?

- Are there parts of the gown I like and parts I don't like? For example, do I like the silhouette, but not the fabric? Do I like the beading, but dislike the neckline? (You should love every part of your dress!)

- Is there a bow or flower on it that I don't like? (If so, ask if it can be sent separately.)

- Is it within my budget?

- Does it fit in with my look?

- Does it help tell my story?

- Can I see myself walking down the aisle in this gown?

- Is this the gown of my dreams?

Managing Your Expectations

A bridal appointment can certainly bring its share of elation or disappointment. Try your best to manage your emotions and expectations. Stay on task: Remember, you're there to find the right dress. Try not to lose focus and let other people or your own emotions spoil your appointment.

While you're standing there on the pedestal, looking at your dress in the mirror, you may have some of the following questions:

What happens if you put on the dress of your dreams and it doesn't look right?
It's not working on you, even though it looked so good in the photograph!

First, it's important not to panic. Don't be afraid to speak up and ask for whatever you need or tell the consultant if you feel uncomfortable or concerned. Be open to your consultant's suggestions. She may be able to offer a solution to help make this your perfect dress. This is also when you should start to explore other silhouettes and styles you may not have considered. This is when you should ask your consultant to choose a dress for you and see what she brings in. You never know. It could turn out to be the perfect dress you never thought of!

Believe me when I tell you, "You will find your dress!" I haven't had a bride walk down the aisle naked yet!

What if you like a dress that is nothing like what you thought?
When a bridal consultant shows you different dress options you may not have considered, don't immediately reject them. What if the gown you write off without a second thought turns out to

WHOSE GOWN IS IT, ANYWAY?

One day I heard a mother down the hall at the salon screaming while her daughter tried on dresses! "Randy! We need you!" she was yelling. "We've got a *huge* problem here!"

Of course, I laughed. "There are no problems here, only challenges," I said. "How may I help you?" She looked completely distraught.

"I love one dress and my daughter likes another one," the mother of the bride said.

I smiled and gently said, "That's not a problem. Who's walking down the aisle?"

The mother of the bride almost seemed insulted. I felt bad for a moment. I certainly didn't mean to insult her. So I cautiously asked her to describe her own outfit to me. She warmed right back up. She then went into a five-minute de-scription of a couture gown she was having custom-made by a designer. She described the drape, the cut, the fabric, the silhouette, the color, and all the accessories

When she finished with her oration, I politely and softly said, "Do you see how excited you get describing your gown to me?" Then I asked her, "How does it make you feel?"

Now she was really smiling. "It makes me feel beautiful!" she exclaimed.

"That's how your daughter needs to feel about her gown," I said.

In the end, the mother took my advice and let her daughter choose the gown she loved.

be the one that flatters you the most? Try to keep an open mind. Don't make judgments about any garment too hastily. Leave yourself open to the chance that a dress may take you by surprise. Go with it. If your response is a positive one, you should put that dress into your "maybe" pile. It may be a keeper! I often have brides who end up purchasing a gown they would have never thought of trying on, because the gown simply made them feel beautiful.

What do you do if you step into your dream gown for the first time, and it just doesn't fit?
It can be hard to envision yourself in a gown when it doesn't fit properly. Often brides can become discouraged when they try on dresses and this happens.

Because bridal gowns are carried in a sample size, it may be hard to imagine what it will look like when it's in the right size and fits correctly.

Try to keep an open mind when trying on sample-size wedding gowns and look beyond the fit of the gown. Remember, this is why your gown will need alterations.

(For more information on alterations, see chapter 8.)

What if you don't fall in love with any dresses?
Again, don't panic. Maybe you need to reschedule another appointment with a clear head and a new direction. You may need to go home, do some more research, pull some other dress styles to consider, and try again.

One thing I will tell you is that you should *never* feel pressured to buy! A good consultant should never have to *sell* you a wedding gown. Once you find the perfect dress, you will know it and be ready to purchase it.

One thing I will tell you is that you should *never* feel pressured to buy!
A good consultant should never have to *sell* you a wedding gown.

Rhonda never thought she'd end up with a gown with ruffles!

The Indecisive Bride

In my experience, sometimes a bride can't say yes to a dress even when everything is perfect and she loves the gown! I often ask what she does for a living. I find that most of the time she has a career that demands analytical thinking. She may tell me she's a doctor, a lawyer, an accountant—a profession where she has to think through every detail thoroughly. Chances are she is overanalyzing the gown. I ask her my usual question, "How do you feel?" She answers, "I like the bodice of this gown," or "I like the way the other gown does this," or "I think this gown will be better for this reason…" Again, I ask her, "How do you *feel*?" I try to get her to connect to the gown with her emotional side instead of her analytical side. I know that if a bride *feels* beautiful in a gown, she will wear it differently. When you feel beautiful in a gown, you stand taller, pose differently, and even walk differently. I know that when a bride feels beautiful, her whole body language changes. People at her wedding will say, "What a beautiful bride!" And it's not just because the dress is beautiful, it's because she *owns* the dress!

RANDY RULE #11

You should *always* purchase the gown that makes you feel the most beautiful!

RHONDA AND TOMA'S STORY

Rhonda, a pediatrician, and her fiancé Toma, an attorney, both consider themselves conservative, methodical, and somewhat conventional. They met through friends at a sports party, but their first official date was at church. When Toma proposed and Rhonda accepted, a very long list was made: the wedding to-do list. Of course, on that list was the wedding dress Rhonda imagined for herself, a dress that reflected everything she was: simple, understated, and, in her words, sort of plain.

Or at least that's the dress she thought would be her dress.

When Rhonda and her more spontaneous sister went bridal gown shopping, the plan began to shift a bit. Rhonda was thrown off guard when her sister suggested she try on a beautiful ruffled dress. Rhonda conceded. What's the worst thing that could happen if she tried it on?

"I put on the ruffles to make my sister happy. When I looked over at my sister, she started to tear up. 'You have to get that dress,' my sister said.

Everyone in the store was telling me that was the dress. The dress gave me the confidence to take a risk and show my more romantic and softer side. It was the dress!

"As I approached the altar, I saw Toma standing there, beaming. As I stepped up to Toma, the pastor nodded at me. I saw them both mouth the words they loved the dress. I had to laugh. They loved the dress!"

Believe me. Rhonda was hardly a plain bride, not by a long shot.

What if you're stuck between two dresses? This one is easy! I ask the same question: "Which gown makes you feel the most beautiful?" You have to like one gown more than another. If a bride tells me she likes both gowns equally, which I simply don't believe, I tell her to buy the less expensive one! It's that simple. That's usually when she confesses to me that she likes one more than the other. Ladies, it should be that simple. Don't overcomplicate the process. I say, "You should *always* go with the gown that makes you feel the most beautiful!"

Some brides get stalled at the appointment because no matter how wonderful a dress looks on them, they believe there will be another gown out there they are missing.

Ladies, you are right! There will *always* be another dress. Every day a designer is creating a new style. Every week the salon receives a new shipment. Yes, there will always be another gown out there. But I say, "Finding a gown is like finding a guy. There will always be another guy out there as well, but at some point you have to stop looking and commit to just one." I say, "You can't go to the singles bar once you get engaged, and you have to stop looking once you've said yes to your dress!"

This is one of those moments you have to make a choice. You're a woman now. It's time to rise to the occasion! Be decisive!

Making Changes to Your Gown

Sometimes you will want to make changes to your gown. There are quite a few changes that you can make. However, I wouldn't recommend buying a gown that requires too many changes. I would also be leery of consultants who promise you that a lot of changes can be made to your gown only to make a sale. If you have to make too many changes to your gown, maybe it's not the right gown for you. You won't be happy at your fitting if your gown cannot be changed.

SWATCHES

Sometimes brides want a swatch of their bridal dress fabric. Fabric shades can vary from bolt to bolt. Your swatch should be used as a guide, and not an exact match for what color the dress may actually come in. Also, the lining color can change the color of your gown.

If you have to make too many changes to your gown, maybe it's not the right gown for you.

TYPES OF GOWN ALTERATIONS

Here are some *possible* changes that a few designers will make to a gown when you order it, and some that can be made during alterations. Make sure you ask your consultant. Remember, there will likely be a charge for any change you make. Again, I caution brides not to make too many changes. Think carefully about making dress changes unless you can easily visualize how they will look.

1. ALTER THE NECKLINE
You can usually raise the neckline or dip it.

2. RAISE THE NECKLINE AND OPEN THE CUP FOR A FULLER BUST
Usually, moderate-priced dress designers do not make any changes to the bustline of a gown. Generally, more expensive dress designers will make bust changes. In order for a dress to accommodate a fuller bust, the designer is required to make a full pattern change. One way to do this is by opening up the princess seam on a dress. This is called opening a cup. Raising the neckline of a gown can also help accommodate a fuller bust. Opening a cup on a dress usually costs around $200 to $400. Raising a neckline can cost anywhere from $100 to $300. For a *very* full bust, you may have to raise the neckline *and* open the cup.

3. CHANGE OR ADD SLEEVES
Sleeves can usually only be added if the gown is made on the shoulder or has an armhole. If a gown already has a sleeve, you can usually have it shortened, lengthened, or even removed.

4. ADD STRAPS
Adding a strap or cap sleeve is a common alteration that can usually be made. Make sure extra fabric is ordered for this when you purchase the dress.

5. CHANGE FABRIC ON THE GOWN
Be careful when changing fabric of a gown. It may change the drape or the way it fits the body.

6. ADD OR REMOVE BOWS, FLOWERS, OR APPLIQUÉS TO THE DRESS
If you do not like a bow, flower, or applique, have it sent separately. You have already paid for it. You may change your mind and decide the gown looks too plain when it comes in without it. You can also purchase a belt or sash to easily change the look of a gown.

7. EXTEND THE TRAIN
Designers usually charge by the foot to extend the train of a gown. Be sure to see how the train will look bustled if you are making it longer. Instead of extending the train, you may decide to wear a longer veil. It will be less expensive and weigh less. (Remember, you will be carrying the weight of that long train bustled up most of the night. It can get heavy.)

8. ADD OR REMOVE CRINOLINE TO THE PETTICOAT
Adding or removing crinoline or netting to make your skirt less poofy or fuller is an easy change that can be made during alterations.

9. CHANGE THE COLOR OF THE GOWN
Gowns come in many different shades of white, ivory, blush, taupe, champagne, and so on. Ask to see a swatch before making your final decision.

What if you say *no* to the dress?

If you have *not* said yes to a dream dress yet, then you may need to start the process over again. Figure out why the dresses you tried on did or did not work out for you. Did you just run out of time? Did you see enough dresses? Did you see too many dresses and got confused? Did you have the right people with you at your appointment to help you make your decision?

Some girls tell me they love a dress in the fitting room, but if their family doesn't react positively, then they can doubt their decision making. "I love it but my mom didn't get excited." Was your consultant right for you? Did you fall in love with a dress that was more than you want to spend? Do you need to adjust your dress budget? Did the salon not have the selection you expected? Do you think you may want to visit a different salon?

Don't get discouraged to start over again. Sometimes it takes a bit longer to find your dream dress.

Again, I promise you will find it!

Saying *Yes* to Your Dress

Saying yes to your dress is sometimes one of the most challenging things for a bride to do. How do you know the dress on your body is really destined for your wedding? Do you cry or get butterflies in your tummy? Remember, every girl reacts differently. What I notice most often when a girl finds her dress is that she simply doesn't want to take it off. She wants to stand in the dress and look at it in the mirror...forever.

So you're standing in front of the mirror and asking yourself, "Is this the one?" This is where you go back to the five essentials. Ask yourself all the important questions:

- Does this dress help tell my story?

- Does it take my story in a new direction? (Remember the story of my bride who got married in a barn? You never know what kind of dress you will end up with.)

- Is this dress within my budget?

- Does this dress suit my location?

- Does it fit in with my look?

What I notice most often when a girl finds her dress is that she simply doesn't want to take it off. She wants to stand in front of the mirror...forever.

Enjoy your bridal appointment!

Crystal's beaded gown required a hollow-to-hem measurement.

You can ask yourself a million questions, but there's really only one question you need to ask yourself, so I will repeat it again:

Which dress makes me feel the most beautiful?

When you look at a dress and ask yourself how you feel, you should answer:

Beautiful...

When you answer that question positively, you have found "the one."

Since I don't get to go to every wedding, this moment is *very* personal for me.

This is the moment when I match a woman with the *perfect* gown. So as you're standing on the pedestal, about to commit to the dress, remember that I am there with you. I understand what an emotional moment this can be. I know some of you have waited your whole life dreaming of this. Some of you are overcome with emotions you didn't expect. Some girls cry. Some don't cry.

You don't have to explain your feelings. For every bride, it will be different. But every girl *knows* when it's right.

GETTING MEASURED

Now that you have found your dress, it's time for you to get measured. This is an important step of the process where you should be able to trust the professional you are working with. A seamstress will come to the fitting room and usually take measurements for your bust, waist, and hips.

The seamstress will order your wedding dress based on your largest measurement: bust, hips, or waist. For example, if your hips and waist are a size 10 but your bust is a 12, you'll get the dress that matches the largest size you need. The other parts of the dress will be taken in to fit your body in alterations.

Hollow-to-hem
It is crucial that your precise measurements be taken before a gown is ordered. Bridal gowns are meant to have a close fit to the body. If a gown has beading all down the front, or if you are a petite bride, you may need a measurement called hollow-to-hem. This measurement is from the hollow of your neck to the hem of the gown. This measurement is also necessary if you are petite and ordering a trumpet or mermaid silhouette. If the gown comes in too long, the flare will fall below your knees and you won't be able to walk in your gown. Keep in mind that there is generally a charge for this measurement since it requires a pattern change. The cost is usually around 10 to 15 percent of the price of the gown. If the gown has a lace scallop or a beaded appliqué at the hem, it can sometimes be ordered separately so you won't have to incur this charge. Ask your consultant or the seamstress who is measuring you.

FINE PRINT AND FINANCIALS

After you've chosen the dress and been measured, you should:

- Read and review the fine print of your order and contract.

- Be very clear about exactly what changes you have asked to be made.

- Make sure that *all* changes, along with prices, you discussed with your consultant are clearly written on your order! When your gown comes in, many months will have passed and you may not remember exactly what was agreed upon.

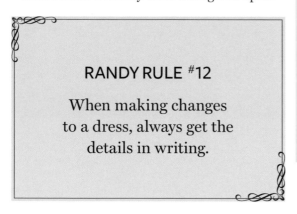

RANDY RULE #12

When making changes to a dress, always get the details in writing.

Your contract should include:

- The designer, style, size, and color of the dress.

- Itemized prices for the dress, accessories, and alterations.

- Estimated delivery dates.

- Exchange and cancellation policies.

You may want to take a photo of the gown with changes noted so you have it for reference at your first fitting.

Are you ready to pay? Most salons require a 50 to 60 percent deposit when the dress is ordered. I would not recommend paying all the money up front for your dress, unless you leave with the gown.

Congratulations! You made it through your appointment and found the gown of your dreams. That is a real accomplishment! You should be proud of yourself.

Now it's time to accessorize!

You may want to take a photo of the gown with changes noted so you have it for reference at your first fitting.

Randy's Recap

TO GET READY FOR YOUR APPOINTMENT, GATHER PHOTOS

•

SELECT THE RIGHT SALON FOR YOU

•

DURING THE APPOINTMENT, COMMUNICATE WITH YOUR CONSULTANT

•

IT MAY BE CHALLENGING, BUT YOUR APPOINTMENT SHOULD BE FUN!

•

YOU SHOULD TRUST YOUR STORY AND YOURSELF

•

CHOOSE THE DRESS THAT MAKES YOU *FEEL* THE MOST BEAUTIFUL

•

ASK ABOUT ANY CHANGES YOU MAY WISH TO MAKE
TO YOUR PARTICULAR GOWN

•

DO NOT GET DISCOURAGED IF YOU DON'T FIND A DRESS AT YOUR
FIRST APPOINTMENT; YOU CAN BEGIN THE PROCESS AGAIN

•

PAY ATTENTION TO THE CONTRACT AND YOUR ORDER: MAKE SURE ALL
CHANGES ARE PUT IN WRITING

•

YOU FOUND YOUR DRESS! ENJOY!

AMY AND MARTIN'S *Story*

Hometown	Los Angeles, California
Wedding Date	May 30
Location	The Athenaeum, Pasadena, California
Wedding Guests	180
Dress Designer	Monique Lhuillier

This was the wedding dress appointment for the record books! It took one year, five states, more than a dozen dress-shopping companions, and hundreds of dresses for Amy to find the right gown for her special day. A fashion, beauty, and bridal editor for a weekly magazine, Amy seemed to have an advantage in the wedding dress search. Instead, she found herself increasingly flustered. "As the search continued I felt more self-conscious, like nothing would ever look good on me. Either my bust was too big or my torso wasn't long enough or I just felt fat. I knew I wanted lace, and I loved Monique Lhuillier, but for some reason I got really sidetracked."

But then, Amy says, a friend got married, and that helped her to refocus the dress search again. Amy spotted a photograph online: the Monique Lhuillier dress she'd been dreaming about! "Randy instantly understood how disillusioned I'd become. I had been to his salon four times already trying on dress after dress! So when he found me the Monique Lhuillier gown that was just right, I felt a strong connection to him. The only disappointment was that after this long process, my parents weren't there to see my dress. Randy understood that, too! He got on the phone with my dad and tried explaining to him how to set up his webcam so he could see me in the dress. Unfortunately my dad couldn't figure it out. So Randy took photos of me in my dress and e-mailed them to my parents. Luckily they were able to open the attachments. I will always remember how Randy went that extra mile for me."

Amy put on that lace dress and added the beaded belt and I just knew. I said, "How do you feel in that dress?" The answer was obvious. The smile on Amy's face gave me the answer. Well, that and the credit card she was holding out for Debbie, her consultant! Amy said, "My mother-in-law loaned me all of her amazing jewelry including Van Cleef & Arpels diamond studs and her antique Edwardian diamond necklace. Her daughter had worn that necklace to her wedding, too, and I always knew I wanted to wear it on my big day. I just needed the right neckline on my dress to show off the necklace! I was so glad to finally find it in the dress I chose."

After trying on hundreds of dresses, Amy knew this was the one!

CHAPTER SEVEN

YOUR *ACCESSORIES*

Accessories will either elevate or depreciate your look. Choose them wisely!

You've found your perfect dress. Now you need to find the perfect accessories to complete the look you've envisioned for your wedding. Here are the accessories you may consider from head to hem: headpiece, veil, jewelry, gloves, cover-ups, shoes, and other essentials—makeup, hair, and bouquet.

Every bride's look is different, and it is with accessories that you refine your look and your theme. Give them some thought. Choosing the perfect earrings, a statement brooch, or an elegant bracelet can often complete or even change your entire bridal look! Accessories also provide you with a chance to add something unexpected to your look, whether it's a jeweled butterfly for your hair or red stilleto shoes. Let your accessories tell your story.

The Veil

A veil is one of the most important accessories a bride can wear. The history of the veil is steeped in tradition. Many of my brides tell me that the moment I place a veil on their head, they feel like brides. It pulls everything together. The type of veil you choose can make all the difference in your look.

Length

What length veil are you looking for? There are many choices, but a long veil should extend approximately 12 to 18 inches past the train. Here's a list of the most common veils, from short to long:

CAGE VEIL

A very short veil that usually attaches to a comb that comes forward and covers half or all of the face, generally made of wide French netting or tulle. It can be associated with a stylized, vintage, or retro look.

ELBOW-LENGTH VEIL

Ends at the elbow or waist. This veil can be poofy, and it looks great when worn with a very full skirt.

FINGERTIP-LENGTH VEIL

Cups right under the bride's hips just past the fingertips. It is one of the most versatile lengths—you can wear it all night, and it goes with just about every style of gown.

WALTZ-LENGTH VEIL

Stops at the floor; usually worn with a long gown that is floor-length.

CHAPEL-LENGTH VEIL

Measures twelve to eighteen inches past a chapel train.

CATHEDRAL-LENGTH VEIL

Measures twelve to eighteen inches past a cathedral train.

FOLD-OVER VEIL

One piece of material that is folded over. It can be short or long, raw or edged. The top layer of tulle can be pulled over your face and used as a blusher (see blushers, page 156).

The right veil can finish off your look.

Fabric

Most veils are made of tulle, although some can also be made of other fabrics like chiffon, lace, or organza.

Edging

The edge of your veil can be left raw (with no edging or hem) or trimmed with fabric, beading, ribbon, lace, or embroidery. As a general rule, the veil should coordinate with and complement the style of your dress. For instance, if you have a beaded dress, you may opt for a beaded veil. If you have a pleated or ruched dress, you may choose a fabric-edged veil. When in doubt, you can never go wrong with a simple, raw-edged veil. It's less expensive and keeps your look clean.

Lace-edged Veils

The mantilla is a Spanish-style veil that frames the face and is edged with lace or made entirely from lace. It is usually worn on the top or the crown of the head and gives the bride a stylized look. When choosing a lace-edged veil, however, consider the fact that heavy lace edging around your face may take away from your natural beauty. I prefer a lace-edged veil where the lace starts at the elbow or fingertip so it looks cleaner around the face, neck, and shoulders.

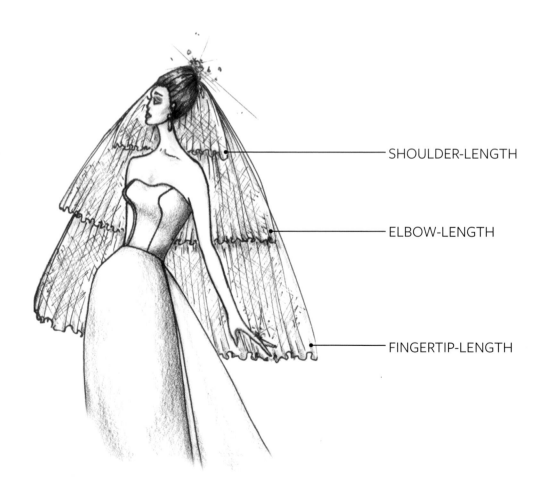

SHOULDER-LENGTH

ELBOW-LENGTH

FINGERTIP-LENGTH

HOW TO BUSTLE A VEIL

You don't want to be caught tripping over your veil while dancing at your wedding. Be sure your bridesmaid or maid of honor knows exactly how to bustle your cathedral or chapel veil. Someone will have to help you with this.

HERE'S HOW:

1. FOLD THE VEIL IN HALF LENGTHWISE.

2. THEN FOLD IT INTO THIRDS AND LIFT IT UP TO THE TOP OF YOUR HEAD.

3. PLACE THAT ON THE TOP OF THE VEIL BASE AND SECURE IT WITH A SIMPLE HAT PIN. THE VEIL SHOULD FALL AROUND YOUR FINGERTIPS.

4. DANCE THE NIGHT AWAY!

CREATE YOUR OWN WEDDING TRADITION

I knew a bride whose veil had been worn by thirteen women in her family. Each woman who wore the veil wrote the date and a few lines about her wedding and placed the veil back into a box. By the time my bride was wed, this box was literally falling apart because it had been traveling around the family for thirty-plus years!

Don't have a veil or piece of jewelry like this in your family? I suggest you start your own tradition. Invest in a gorgeous veil or piece of jewelry. Purchase a journal and nice box to store the object. On your wedding day, write in the journal about the piece and what it means to you. Then pass the heirloom along to your family and loved ones for their

weddings and special occasions. One day, someone will open that box and discover a journal filled with a lifetime of stories that all started with yours.

Blushers

Blushers lightly cover the face of the bride. They are mysterious and traditional—they give the father or groom a moment to lift the veil literally and figuratively to see the beauty once the ceremony has begun. Legend says that the groom would lift a veil to make certain he'd married the right sister! Also, it's believed that the eyes are windows to the soul. The groom would lift the veil and be the first person to look into the bride's eyes and capture her heart and soul.

If you choose or if religion dictates that you must wear a blusher, then I say go for it! Consider a long blusher that goes down in front, past your hands and the bouquet you are holding. This longer blusher will give you a chic, sophisticated, and more dramatic look.

If you are wearing a blusher, you should have your father or groom *practice* lifting it before the actual wedding. You need to make sure that you anticipate anything that might catch on the veil or prevent it from being lifted properly.

Where do I wear my veil?

Consider your hairstyle—the veil can rest in the style, under a bun, et cetera.

Typically, a veil should start at the crown of a bride's head. That placement will make the bride look taller.

For brides who really don't want to wear a veil, consider this chic and understated option: Try wearing your veil under a low chignon, secured well with pins, and go long with its length. This gives you the drama of the veil without feeling like it overpowers your head.

There are certain measurements for specific veil lengths. I don't rely on measurements, however, because I feel the length of a veil should be in proportion to a bride's height, where she's wearing it on her head, and the style of her gown.

If you wear a straight, slim dress, then consider a long, slim veil that reinforces the gown's vertical silhouette. A poofy ball gown may look best with a shorter poofy veil.

If you are having an outdoor wedding, be sure to consider a veil with a little weight or extra length. If the wind is blowing, the veil could sweep over your face and smudge your makeup…we don't want that.

RANDY RULE #13

Without a veil, you're just a pretty girl in a white dress.

The Headpiece

Brides are finding more and more options to add sparkle, shimmer, and drama to their ensembles. One of the favorite places to do this is with a headpiece. A headpiece is a wonderful accessory because it brings attention to the bride's beautiful face and hair. It can be worn throughout the night, even if you decide to remove your veil, and still makes you stand out. A headpiece reminds everyone that you're the bride.

Headpieces may be adorned with jewels, flowers, beads, feathers, or combinations of all these elements. Your headpiece should coordinate with and complement your dress color, style, and embellishment. You should *always* consider your hairstyle when choosing your headpiece. How you wear your hair will help determine which headpiece you choose. Whether your hair is worn down, pulled up, or half up and half down, most headpieces can be worn with any hairstyle.

Even though crowns and tiaras can be quite popular, I would rather you invest in a jeweled headband or crystal pin that can be worn again rather than a tiara or crown that is really better suited for a pageant winner. You can wear hair jewelry long after the wedding for a special occasion like your anniversary. You may even hand this accessory down to future generations as your own wedding "heirloom."

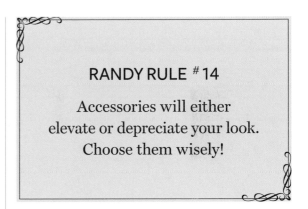

RANDY RULE #14

Accessories will either elevate or depreciate your look. Choose them wisely!

Some brides choose fabric or even fresh flowers for their hair. However, if you are using real flowers, have a backup set of fresh ones in case the first set starts to wilt. Here are some attractive headpieces:

COMB

Attached to the head with comb teeth.

CROWN

A circular headpiece that sits on the crown of the head.

TIARA

A half-crown or semicircle that sits on the crown of the head.

HEADBAND

A band that stays snug on the head.

HAIR JEWELRY

Tied with ribbon or hooked with a metal piece to the back of the neck.

HAIR PINS

Pins placed into the hairstyle.

Jill has chosen ear-
rings, a bracelet,
and a brooch. Each
piece is different,
yet works well with
the others.

Jewelry

Jewelry can be anything from a simple pair of diamond stud earrings to a sentimental pearl necklace worn by your grandmother. Jewelry should complement your gown style. Everything needs to be harmonious and be in proportion to all of the other elements of your look.

I usually prefer a bride without a necklace because I feel that it gives her a cleaner, longer look and it does not compete with her face or the bodice of the dress. Your jewelry should have the same feeling and formality as your gown, and all the pieces should be in proportion and work together. Be careful not to wear too much jewelry. You want jewelry to enhance your look, not overpower it! However, if your gown has huge crystals on the bodice, a small pair of earrings will get lost. As a personal preference, I like some kind of crystal to help a girl with blue eyes to sparkle! When it comes to jewelry, remember it all comes down to proportion and quality.

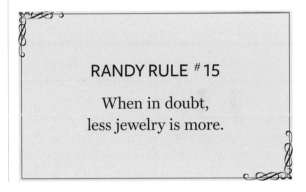

RANDY RULE #15

When in doubt,
less jewelry is more.

Linique chose to wear
a bracelet that had
sentimental value to her.

THE SENTIMENTAL ACCESSORY

If you have an article that has personal meaning for you, like your great-grandmother's brooch or your mother's veil—anything that is valuable to you emotionally—I feel that object does not have to match everything else in your ensemble.

I meet many brides who are worried about including a sentimental accessory or veil because they feel it doesn't "go with" everything else. People at your wedding will realize why you have included a sentimental item in your wedding look; they will appreciate and respect you for honoring its sentimental value. Your sentimental accessory enhances your story and makes your wedding even richer and more personal.

Shoes

When accessorizing head-to-hem, don't forget the all-important shoe. As with all other accessories that you have chosen, shoes need to continue the look and feel of your wedding outfit.

For instance, with a delicate dress, you might choose a light, strappy shoe. For a formal wedding gown, consider a satin pump, something embroidered—or what about a sparkling crystal-covered heel?

If you want to add a little color to your wedding, a shoe can be the ideal place to do this. It's not something that will overpower your look; it can peek out throughout the wedding, giving guests a glimpse of color as you walk down the aisle or while you dance at the reception.

I have to say that I prefer when a woman wears a pair of heels. When you wear a heel, you stand taller. Heels give you a feminine and sexy swagger when you walk. In a pair of flats, you tend to walk "flat." And I know I said that every rule has its exception, but here's one rule that for me has no exceptions: Never, ever wear flip-flops with your wedding gown. Even if you have a beach wedding, I would rather see you in an elegant pair of sandals, foot jewelry, or barefoot with a pretty pedicure. If you absolutely must wear a flat shoe, then go with something pretty like a ballet slipper. Please don't cheapen your bridal look with a pair of rubber flip-flops that will make a snapping sound when you walk.

I also recommend that a bride have a backup pair of shoes on hand in case a heel or strap breaks on your first pair. The second pair does not need to be the same style, but it should have the same heel height. Your gown will be hemmed and bustled to a certain length; you want to maintain that length so it doesn't drag on the floor.

I would rather a bride invest in a good-quality pair of shoes she can wear again than spend money on an inexpensive shoe she will dispose of after the wedding is over. Get a pair you love and get use out of them. You can always wear those shoes on your anniversaries!

I would rather a bride invest in a good-quality pair of shoes
she can wear again than spend money on an inexpensive shoe
she will dispose of after the wedding is over.

Rhonda chose a pair of sexy, jeweled, peep-toe shoes!

Shoshanna's wedding followed Orthodox Jewish tradition: She could not show her shoulders during the wedding. We ordered extra French Alençon lace fabric that matched her gown and made a custom bolero jacket.

Cover-Ups

If the weather will be cold during your wedding or if you have to cover your shoulders or arms because of your religion, then consider a cover-up so you can still wear the strapless dress of your dreams.

When wearing a cover-up, you should consider going *light* on the fabric. For any cover-up, be sure that you have range of movement. The last thing you want is to raise your arms and be unable to reach something because your sleeve is tight.

Here are a few options for beautiful cover-ups:

BOLERO

A short jacket, with or without sleeves, that falls no longer than the waistline. Of Spanish origin, this type of jacket is worn open in front over the bodice of the gown.

CAPELET

A small cape that is worn over the shoulders.

COAT

A sleeved outer garment that extends from the shoulders to the waist or below.

FUR (REAL OR FAUX)

A garment, neckpiece, stole, or jacket made of or lined with the fur of a mammal. The "fur" piece can be made of faux-fur material.

JACKET

A sleeved hip- or waist-length garment that covers the upper body.

SHAWL

A square or oblong garment used as a covering for the shoulders or carried on the arm.

SHRUG

A small jacket that falls above the waistline, usually shorter than a bolero.

STOLE

A wide scarf, usually made of an expensive fabric, that is worn about the shoulders.

WRAP

Any garment that wraps around the body for warmth.

Gloves

As a general rule, I am not a big fan of gloves. A long glove usually stops at the widest part of your arm and breaks up the long, clean line.

If you decide that you want gloves because they *do* elevate your look or for a vintage feel, then consider wearing gloves in opera length (ends between the elbow and shoulder) made from a fine fabric or a soft kid leather. Don't wear the stark white shiny polyester ones! It will only depreciate your look.

But remember, if you *do* choose to wear a glove, you will have to remove it during the ceremony to put on your wedding ring. You can wear gloves for photographs and then take them off before the ceremony.

Some brides wear their hair up for the ceremony and let it down for the reception.

HAIR, MAKEUP, AND MANICURE

You will have a photographer taking your photograph all day. You need to wear makeup that looks natural and highlights your beauty.

One of the most important points about your makeup is the time of your wedding. You need to consider how a bright flash at night or bold sunlight will make you look. Consult with a makeup stylist at a salon or a makeup counter. Do a trial run with your makeup before the wedding.

As with all accessories, your hair is an important part of your complete look. It should complement the shape of your face and should not compete with your gown's neckline, jewelry, or veil.

In the same way that you chose photographs of your favorite dresses, gather photographs of hairstyles you like best. After you do a trial hair-styling appointment, be sure to take a photograph of the style you choose. This way, you have something to show your hairstylist on your wedding day. Remember that your hairstylist works with many clients a day; by the date of your wedding, he or she may have forgotten your specific hairstyle.

And please remember how important your hands are on the wedding day . . . for rings and embraces. Get a manicure, making sure the color complements your look.

Your hairstyle should flatter your face and complement your overall look.

Shorter stems on a bouquet will allow you to carry it tilted down so your guests can admire its beauty.

The Right Bouquet

A beautiful bouquet of flowers should highlight the bride's face, makeup, and of course her dress. Don't choose the colors of your bouquet just because they're your favorite colors. I prefer that you choose flowers that complement and are in the same tones as your makeup and skin.

If you are very pale and you wear light makeup, don't choose bright red roses for your bouquet. When walking down the aisle, that pop of color will be all your guests will see. Choose a paler pink or cream.

When I say that your bouquet should not be bigger than your head, I'm talking about proportion. A bride with a small head will look awkward carrying an enormous, heavy bouquet. If you're delicate and petite, your flowers should be on the same scale. If you have a fuller figure, a bouquet that is fuller will be a better proportion for you. If your gown is very sleek and architectural in style, then your floral arrangement should echo that style. If the top of the dress is delicate lace, then choose lacy flowers.

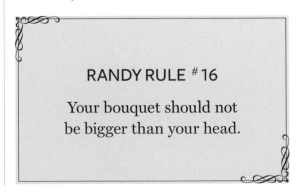

RANDY RULE # 16

Your bouquet should not
be bigger than your head.

Amy and I having
fun on set tossing
the bouquet!

Something Old, Something New, Something Borrowed, Something Blue

Here are a few of my brides' favorites:

OLD

- Your grandmother's veil
- Antique earrings or bracelet
- A vintage clutch
- The buttons from your mother's wedding dress
- A locket hanging from your bouquet with a portrait of a loved one who has passed
- A piece of lace or fabric from your mother's gown sewn to the underside of your dress

NEW

- Your dress (of course)
- Lingerie
- Chic, fabulous shoes
- Diamond earrings from your fiancé (or his parents)
- A silk velvet shawl (for a fall or winter wedding)

BORROWED

- The earrings your grandmother wore at her wedding
- Your friend's bracelet
- An elegant wrap from your future mother-in-law

BLUE

- Blue flowers in your bouquet, such as hydrangeas
- Blue crystals spelling your initials glued under the arch of your shoes
- Tiny blue details, such as flowers, scattered on a long veil
- Your and your fiancé's names, initials, or wedding date embroidered on the inside of your gown

Jessica had lace from her mother's wedding gown sewn to the lining of her gown.

THE VERY BEST ACCESSORY OF ALL: YOUR GROOM

Don't forget your groom. He's your most important accessory! I'll talk more about him in chapter 9.

Randy's Recap

THERE ARE MANY STYLES OF VEILS, HEADPIECES, AND ACCESSORIES
YOU WILL CHOOSE FOR A WEDDING. HOWEVER,
THERE ARE REALLY ONLY FIVE THINGS YOU NEED TO ASK
WHEN SELECTING *ANY* ACCESSORY:

IS IT IN PROPORTION?

•

DOES IT TELL MY STORY?

•

IS IT A SENTIMENTAL ITEM?

•

DOES IT COMPLEMENT MY LOOK?

•

DOES IT ELEVATE MY LOOK?

SUSAN AND BRUCE'S *Story*

Hometown	Long Island, New York
Wedding Date	June 20
Location	De Seversky Du Pont Mansion, Long Island, New York
Wedding Guests	75
Dress Designer	Pnina Tornai

For the second time, Susan was engaged to be married. Her fiancé was a family friend with whom she'd begun a relationship nearly twenty years earlier. In what seemed like the middle of their relationship, they were starting anew. She and Bruce wanted to say, "I do!"

At first, Susan considered Bruce's proposal very practically. She would wear a plain-colored dress or even a suit for their wedding ceremony. But then she turned fifty. And just like that, Susan drafted a bucket list and on top was this: *Shop at a real New York bridal salon for a real wedding dress.* If she was going to marry again, Susan was determined to do it *her* way and to get everything she wanted this time around, including the white dress!

"Since I am not a young woman, I had a certain amount of self-consciousness buying *anything* from a bridal salon. All around me were twenty-somethings and their parents shopping for their dresses. I was the other woman, the older woman. And then I met Randy. 'You're so beautiful!' Randy insisted. 'You can be a beautiful bride at any age!' He was more interested in my story and how a dress might be a reflection of my inner self than he was interested in selling me something."

I remember Susan calling me before her alterations appointment from outside. She was so anxious, she told me she might not be able to make it into the salon. I met her outside, walked her into the salon, and stayed for her fitting. Once she put her dress on, the anxiety disappeared. She looked amazing!

To accessorize her look, Susan wore an incredible choker made of several strands of pearls. One strand came from her mother, and a double strand from her sister. It was as if all the women in her life came alive in her necklace, and she carried them close to her heart on the wedding day.

"Randy called me the night before the wedding and left a message on my answering machine. 'You are elegant and classy and I hope your day is as beautiful as I know you look.' I saved the voice mail he left me that day. I still listen to it and remember him, the dress, and the day. For me, it really *was* a new beginning."

Susan's special accessory was the strands of pearls from her sister and mother worn around her neck.

CHAPTER EIGHT

YOUR *FITTING*

Your dress should fit like a glove

At last you've selected the perfect wedding gown and accessorized your look. You're almost ready for your big day. However, there's one more *very* important step... alterations!

Altering a bridal gown is no simple task! A good seamstress is like an artist. Alterations on a bridal gown are very different from alterations made on other garments.

The construction of a wedding gown can be extremely complex. It usually consists of many layers of fabrics, boning, lace, and beading. Sometimes seamstresses have to cut apart entire bodices of dresses, open and resew seams, create straps or sleeves, hand-bead hundreds of tiny crystals, or invent a bustle where one did not exist before. This requires tremendous skill and craftsmanship. I strongly suggest you choose a skilled seamstress, one who comes highly recommended, and then develop a close relationship with that person.

Why are alterations so important? For most women, your wedding gown may be the closest thing to couture that you will ever wear. We're talking about dropping thousands of dollars on one dress. It will be photographed hundreds of times. All guests' eyes will be on you from the beginning of your wedding to the end.

Simply stated, a gown that is not fitted properly will look cheap and sloppy. Your dress should fit like a glove. Besides, there's nothing worse than watching a bride tugging at her strapless gown all night to keep it from falling down, or tripping on a hem that's too long.

What to Bring to Your Fitting

Being prepared for your alterations appointment and bringing the right items will ensure a more successful fitting for both you and the person doing your alterations. Also, bringing the necessary documents, photos, and accessories can mean fewer fittings, which is definitely a good thing. One photo you may want to be careful bringing to your fitting is the one taken from the magazine of a super-thin model that has been over-airbrushed wearing your gown. Brides often bring these photos to their fitting appointment and become disappointed when they don't look like the girl in the photo. Here are the items I suggest you bring with you to your fitting:

- Bring a copy of your original contract, including written changes agreed upon when you purchased your gown as well as any photos of these changes you may have taken. Your fitter was probably not present when you purchased your gown, so he or she may not be aware of changes that were discussed or promised. This is why those written records and photos I told you to get are so important!

- Bring your shoes if you have purchased them; if you haven't, bring a shoe with the same heel height that you will be wearing on your wedding day. This will allow your seamstress to start working on the hem and bustle at the first fitting.

- Be sure to wear the proper undergarments with your gown, as they will affect the fit. Unless you have a very small bust, or cups are sewn directly into your gown, you will need to wear some kind of bra for support. The style of your gown and your bust size will both help determine which bra or bustier is best for you. Your fitter can also help you choose. Generally your salon or alterations specialist will carry a selection of bras, strapless bras, long-line bras, and bustiers. There are also body shapers and slimmers available that can be used to create a smooth look under a slinky gown. Padded bra cups can be added to fill out and shape your bustline.

- Bring all the accessories that you will be wearing with your gown (headpiece, veil, jewelry, and so on) to your fitting. Be sure to check their color and proportion to make sure they all work together beautifully to accomplish your desired look.

Who to Bring to Your Fitting

As I established in the appointment chapter, the people you bring to your fitting appointment can drastically change what kind of experience you have. Again, I suggest that you bring with you only the people you really need, and who are supportive and have your best interests at heart. This should be someone you trust, like your mother, maid of honor, or a good friend. Too many people looking and commenting on your dress during your fitting can only add anxiety. Be sure to bring along the person who will be in charge of bustling your gown, tying ribbons or bows, helping you get dressed, or helping with the headpiece or veil. They should learn the process and practice *before* the wedding.

Your First Fitting

Generally your gown arrives approximately two months before the wedding. It should then go through quality control at the salon. This is to confirm that the correct gown has been received, making sure the style, size, fabric, color, and changes (if any were made) are correct, and to check the overall condition of the gown.

Once the gown is approved, customer service will contact you to set up your first fitting appointment around six to eight weeks before your wedding.

If you have not heard from the salon and your wedding day is in less than two months, I would call the salon and check on its delivery status.

I suggest that you bring with you only the people you really need, and who are supportive and have your best interests at heart. This should be someone you trust, like your mother, maid of honor, or a good friend.

RANDY RULE #17

Do not skimp on alterations! Your gown must fit properly!

Okay, ladies, here it is…you are about to see *the* gown you've been dreaming of for the past six to twelve months! *Your* gown! It's at this moment that I see many brides break down emotionally…the moment they see *their* gown for the first time!

It looks different than you remember! That's why you took photos.

The color looks brighter than the one you tried on! This is because the sample was tried on many times before and was therefore slightly darker in color.

It looks huge! That's because they ordered it in the size that accommodates the fullest part of your body.

The bust is huge! The waist is baggy! The length is too long! It doesn't fit! You start to panic. Your heart sinks to your stomach. You begin to perspire. You suddenly feel dizzy. You're about to cry.

Stop!

Remember, this is why it is called a fitting! The time when a bride has her fittings can be one of her most emotional and stressful. She's a few months away from the biggest event in her entire life. Trying to get all the last-minute details together can really be taking its toll on her emotions, and she can easily lash out at the nearest person. Often this person is the one doing the alterations. Some call these brides Bridezillas!

I personally don't believe in Bridezillas. I feel that I have an anxious, young, frightened woman in front of me who just wants to look beautiful on her wedding day. And what's wrong with that? She may simply not have the vocabulary or experience to deal with these affairs. She may have frustration with her family or other outside events going on in her life.

The pressure of all that can turn even the most composed bride into a basket case!

These women may just need a little more love, support, or encouragement during this time.

However, with the tools I am giving you within the pages of this book, I'm ensuring you won't become a Bridezilla.

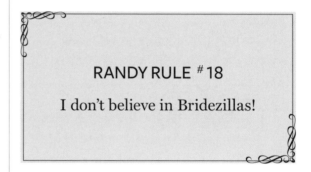

RANDY RULE #18

I don't believe in Bridezillas!

You should definitely check out your gown carefully. Make sure it's the correct style and color, and check for any imperfections. This is your chance to voice your concerns about what you see and express how you feel with regard to your gown. Don't hold back if you feel something is not correct. However, be sure to give your fitter a moment to assess your gown with his or her trained eye. And give them a moment to recommend solutions.

Schedule your second fitting appointment before you leave.

POSSIBLE ALTERATIONS TO DISCUSS AT YOUR FITTING

HERE IS MY LIST OF COMMON ALTERATIONS :

- FITTING YOUR BUST SO YOU'RE NOT EXPOSED WHEN YOU BEND OVER

- LOWERING OR DIPPING THE NECKLINE

- ADDING CUPS TO FILL OUT YOUR BUST

- TAKING IN AND FITTING THE WAIST

- TAKING IN AND FITTING YOUR HIPS

- ADDING STRAPS OR SLEEVES

- ADDING BEADING

- ADDING LACE

- REMOVING SOME OF THE PETTICOAT TO MAKE IT SLIMMER

- ADD NETTING TO THE PETTICOAT TO MAKE IT FULLER

- MAKING A SHRUG OR BOLERO

- HEMMING THE GOWN

PROPER GOWN LENGTH

A bridal gown is at the proper length when the hem just touches the top of your shoe when you step forward. Make sure it doesn't buckle or catch on the floor when you walk. It may appear short to you, but remember, unlike the gowns you see on the red carpet at the Academy Awards that pool on the ground, you will be walking and dancing at your wedding, not just posing for the paparazzi.

HEMMING LACE

The lace scallops can be cut out, raised to the proper length, and reapplied. If it's an all-lace gown, the excess lace will be cut away from underneath after the scallops are sewn back on.

CREATING A BUSTLE FOR THE TRAIN

Your fitter will show you the options for bustling your specific gown. See page 60 for types of bustles. You must have on the shoes you will be wearing at your wedding before your bustle can be finished. I personally feel tulle bustles look bulky and unattractive. If you're wearing a gown with a tulle train, you may consider cutting the train off to make the gown floor-length. Instead, I suggest you wear a long tulle veil or detachable train for added drama when walking down the aisle.

Your Second Fitting

Your second fitting takes place about a month before your wedding. Your gown will now fit your body more closely, and you should be able to easily envision what it is going to look like finished. If you weren't able to bring your shoes with you at your first fitting, then this is when the hem

> You should take your gown for a walk to see if you can comfortably maneuver in it.

and bustle will be pinned to the correct length. Again, take a closer look at your gown and make sure you feel comfortable and it is fitting correctly. You should take your gown for a walk to see if you can comfortably maneuver in it. Can you raise your arms? Can you sit down? Be sure you don't take it in so much that you can't breathe, walk, or sit down. Take a good look in the mirror from all angles. Make sure your bra doesn't show. If it is strapless, make sure it is not slipping down. A strapless dress is held up with boning and interfacing and should be snug at the waist. The gown should be fairly comfortable. There should be nothing scratchy or irritating your skin.

Schedule your third or final fitting before you leave.

Your Third or Final Fitting

The final fitting is usually scheduled fairly close to the wedding date. This is the last time you will have the chance to put your gown on before the wedding, so be sure you are completely happy with the way the gown looks and feels! Speak up and ask questions or voice any concerns about your gown, as this will be your final chance to make any changes. Make sure you bring the person who will be dressing you, bustling your gown, and helping you on your wedding day. Encourage them to practice until they completely understand the process!

Sometimes you can make arrangements with your fitter to attend your wedding to help you get dressed and bustle your gown.

Adjusting Linique's train and French bustle.

Picking Up Your Gown

Final payment will be required, so don't forget your wallet. Your gown should be pressed or steamed, stuffed with tissue to keep its shape, and packed in a large opaque garment bag. Most brides pick up their gowns in a vehicle large enough to lay the dress down without getting it wrinkled. When you get home, be sure to hang it up quickly in a safe place where it won't get wrinkled, disturbed, or damaged.

Preserving or Storing Your Gown

There are a lot of experts who will tell you to have your gown preserved and sealed after your wedding. I have different thoughts. I do agree that you need to have your dress spot-cleaned as soon as possible. The stains and oils from your hands should not be allowed to set. If it were my gown, after a thorough cleaning, I would either hang it in a dark dry place with a sheet over it, or place it in an acid-free box and store it in a cool, dark, dry place. If you have your gown preserved and sealed in a box, you won't be able to take it out from time to time and appreciate it.

TRAVELING WITH YOUR GOWN BY PLANE

Destination weddings are popular. However, traveling on a plane with your gown can be challenging unless it's small and easily packed in a carry-on. Some bridal salons will pack your gown in a suitcase for you. I have even heard of brides buying a ticket for an extra seat just for their gown. Luggage restrictions on airlines change constantly, and they can vary from one airline to another. I highly re-commend checking with your airline on their specific requirements for traveling with your gown before making any travel arrangements.

Make sure to bring to the fitting the person who will be dressing you, bustling your gown, and helping you on your wedding day.

Randy's Recap

A PERFECTLY FITTED GOWN IS A MUST!

•

CHOOSE A SEAMSTRESS WHO IS HIGHLY SKILLED AND DEVELOP
A GOOD RELATIONSHIP WITH THAT PERSON

•

YOUR FIRST FITTING APPOINTMENT SHOULD BE SCHEDULED
SIX TO EIGHT WEEKS BEFORE YOUR WEDDING DATE

•

AT YOUR FIRST FITTING, BE SURE THAT YOUR GOWN IS THE CORRECT
STYLE AND COLOR, AND CHECK FOR ANY IMPERFECTIONS

•

COME PREPARED TO YOUR FITTINGS: BRING ALL THE NECESSARY
ITEMS, INCLUDING SHOES, VEIL, AND ACCESSORIES

•

DESIGNATE SOMEONE TO BE YOUR OFFICIAL "BUSTLER" FOR YOUR
GOWN AND BRING THEM WITH YOU TO YOUR FITTINGS

•

AT YOUR FINAL FITTING APPOINTMENT, MAKE SURE YOU ARE
COMPLETELY SATISFIED WITH THE WAY YOUR
GOWN LOOKS, FEELS, AND FITS

JESSICA AND GREG'S *Story*

Hometown	New York City
Wedding Date	July 24
Location	The Watermill Caterers, Smithtown, Long Island, New York
Wedding Guests	160
Dress Designer	Pnina Tornai

Jessica's fiancé's mother, Rosanne, is the vice president of Kleinfeld and has worked in the bridal industry for almost thirty years. So when Jessica got engaged to Greg, she knew her experience was going to be different from most brides'. Jessica's husband teases her that although the very first gown she tried on was the one she ended up coming back to, she still had to try on hundreds of other gowns just to be sure. (Her mother-in-law encouraged her to keep trying!) Jessica was ready to try on every gown in the salon, but Greg was thinking differently. He was clear: "I don't care what dress it is. Jessica could come down that aisle in a garbage bag and I'll love her just the same."

Jessica had worked in the salon with me and trusted my opinion. I remember her trying on so many gowns, but she kept coming back to the original gown by Pnina Tornai. For the consultants and myself, it's even more exciting when someone we know and care about is searching for their dream dress! "Randy was there the very first time—and the very last time I tried on this gown."

Throughout the process of choosing the dress, Jessica felt calm. Even during her alterations she trusted the team of seamstresses to make her gown fit beautifully. "I remember when Rosanne would visit me during my fittings. I knew she would make sure my gown fit perfectly. Every time she came in, she would tell the fitters what adjustments they needed to make to properly fit my gown. She came in so many times during my fitting that the head of alterations had to politely ask her to leave until they finished. In the end, the gown fit perfectly and Rosanne was allowed to see the final product. Her actions during this process showed me just how much she cared about me and how far she would go to make sure I was happy! I also had my seamstress add some crystal beading to the neckline of my gown. The hand beading gave my gown a little bit of sparkle and made it unique." The final touch Jessica added to her gown during her alterations was having JESSICA & GREG embroidered in blue thread on the lining of the dress.

After careful alteration, Jessica's gown fit perfectly!

CHAPTER NINE

YOUR BRIDESMAIDS, MOTHERS & MEN

Both the wedding party and the groom's attire should complement your dress in look, style, and formality

We know this book is all about *your* dress, but other people at your wedding are dressing up, too. What is your groom wearing? How about your bridesmaids, mothers of the bride and groom, and other members of your bridal party?

I'm not going to go into *too* much detail about what everyone else should wear. That could fill another whole book! However, I will say this: When it comes to selecting attire for your bridal party to wear, I suggest you guide everyone to choose outfits that complement the overall look and story of your wedding. This will help create a cohesive appearance and ensure that everyone fits in.

It's wise to be *very* clear about any desires, goals, and expectations you have from others at your wedding. People will appreciate it, and want direction from you.

There are times when dealing with family during the wedding-planning process can be challenging. But remember, your loved ones truly want the best possible wedding for you. You just need to make sure you're communicating everything *you* want.

Bridesmaids

In the past, being asked to be in a bridal party would conjure up images of frightening, ill-fitting dresses in hideous colors that flattered no one. I remember my girlfriend telling me about a bridesmaid's dress she had to wear. It was in the 1980s, and for bridesmaids' dresses, floral chintz fabric was in! She stepped into the dress, looked at herself in the mirror, and then looked over at the overstuffed floral chintz sofa beside her. Realizing that she looked like a great big floral chintz sofa herself, she sadly broke down crying.

Ladies, remember, your bridesmaids are your friends and loved ones. They will *also* be standing beside you most of your wedding day. *Their* look should complement your story, your plan, and *your* look, and you want them to look good and feel comfortable about what they are wearing, too.

They should be happy to be a part of your wedding celebration...and *not* feel like a floral print sofa!

Today, plenty of bridesmaids' dresses are fresh, unique, and fashionable. There are many styles to choose from that will flatter different body shapes and sizes, and they come in a plethora

RANDY RULE #19

When selecting bridesmaids' dresses, ask yourself, "Would I be happy wearing this?"

Try to choose bridesmaids' gowns that complement your color scheme, overall wedding look, and story.

As a general rule, short dresses lend themselves
to a more informal wedding, and long gowns tend to
give a more formal look.

of colors. Here are some of my suggestions for dressing your bridesmaids:

- Try to choose bridesmaids' gowns that complement your color scheme, overall wedding look, and story.

- Having matching bridesmaids' dresses is a beautiful look and a popular tradition. This works best when all of your maids are the same size and shape. Everyone looks good as a group, and the dresses will look nice in your photographs. Another option is to choose similar style dresses, offering your bridesmaids different silhouettes and necklines in the same color. (No rainbow-colored bridesmaids' dresses, please!) These variations will allow everyone to wear a dress that flatters her body, while maintaining a cohesive look for your wedding.

- As a general rule, short dresses lend themselves to a more informal wedding, and long gowns tend to give a more formal look.

- Order attendants' attire at least four to six months in advance of the wedding. This will allow enough time for everyone to have enough fittings necessary to make sure their dress fits properly.

- Your bridesmaids' shoes should also coordinate. Their shoes may not match exactly, but they should be similar in style and definitely be in the same color.

- Make sure your bridesmaids' shoes are appropriate for the season, the time of day, the setting, and the look of your wedding.

- Choosing bridesmaids' dresses that show off too much cleavage or bare skin is generally not appropriate. Remember, you want your attendants to feel as beautiful as you do, and dresses that are too risqué may make them feel uncomfortable.

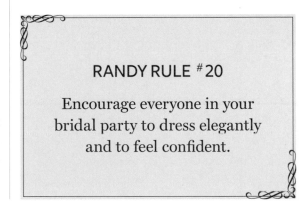

RANDY RULE #20

Encourage everyone in your
bridal party to dress elegantly
and to feel confident.

Mothers

If there ever were a dress that was a challenge to find, I would rank a mother-of-the-bride or -groom dress at the top of my list! Mothers today are quite different from mothers in the past. In general, they are more youthful looking and are taking better care of their bodies. And when it comes to dressing, many are very hip and quite chic.

The challenge for a mother of the bride or groom is finding a dress that is dressy enough for the wedding, but not too flashy. She needs a dress that is special, but one that doesn't outshine the bride's gown. Mothers want to look sexy without being too risqué, and simple and elegant without looking frumpy. Their dress should be special enough to stand next to their son or daughter, but they shouldn't have to spend as much money as the bride did on her gown to achieve this. A lot of mothers today have terrific bodies and want to show them off but still want to be tasteful.

Luckily, there are many choices for the mother of the bride or groom today. Like bridesmaids' dresses, there are more styles, more colors, and more refreshing options. For mothers of the bride and groom, my guidelines are similar to the ones I suggest for helping a bride find *her* gown:

- Shop early! As soon as the bride finds her gown and selects the bridesmaids' colors, the mother of the bride should start looking for her dress. You want to coordinate with the others in the bridal party and not clash with them.

- The couple should speak with their mothers about the details of their wedding. You should be very clear when articulating your story, plan, and look of your wedding. Clear communication is essential to ensure the mothers' gowns will fit in with the overall look and formality of the wedding.

- As a general rule, the mother of the bride sets the tone with her dress for the mother of the groom to follow. For example, if the mother of the bride is wearing a fully beaded gown for the wedding, the mother of the groom should choose something of equal dressiness if possible.

- I suggest mothers compare fabric swatches or photos of their gowns to make sure their gowns complement each other.

- It's more important that the mothers' dresses match in style and formality than color.

- For more formal weddings, beads, sparkling brooches, luxurious fabrics, and full-length gowns are appropriate and acceptable.

- For more informal weddings, you may still wear a full-length gown if it is okay with the bride. However, you should probably steer away from wearing anything too flashy.

- For warmer weather, consider wearing lighter fabrics, in lighter or even brighter colors. Again, check with the couple to see what the overall color scheme for the wedding is.

- For cooler weather, heavier fabrics and richer colors, like jewel tones, can look lovely.

- Out of respect, unless the bride is having an all-white wedding, mothers should *never* wear white!

- It is, however, acceptable for mothers to wear black. I remember in 1996 when my dear friend

Cele Lalli, then editor in chief of *Modern Bride* magazine, wore black to her daughter's wedding. Cele had dark eyes and silver hair and the black gown looked stunning on her!

- Mothers' gowns do not need to be the same length as the bridesmaids' dresses. You may decide to have your bridesmaids wear short dresses, and some mothers may not feel comfortable in a short dress.

- The mothers' own tastes should be taken into consideration as well. Mothers should be able to ask themselves, "How does this dress make me feel?" The answer should be: Beautiful!

- Just as the mother goes with her daughter to shop for her wedding gown, I suggest brides accompany the mothers. This outing can be fun, and it will ensure your moms choose dresses that make you both happy.

- The best advice I have for mothers searching for the perfect dress is the same as for brides searching for their gown. You must *try it on*.

THE MOTHER OF THE BRIDE

When my niece got married, my sister-in-law Marilyn needed a gown to wear as mother of the bride. We scoured every dress shop and department store searching for the perfect dress. We were left empty-handed because she could find nothing that she loved. As I've said, I feel that everyone should have the privilege of feeling beautiful when they are dressed! Finally, I decided to design a gown for her myself.

She was in her early fifties and like most mothers wanted a gown that would show off her great body and look youthful, but not too sexy. I created a full-length form-fitting trumpet gown for her in an apple-green four-ply silk crepe. It was sleeveless, and had a Sabrina neckline. To wear over the simple gown, I designed a very sheer, floor-length flowing silk chiffon coat with a jewel neckline and slim long sleeves, also in apple green. It hooked at the front of the neck with a tiny hook and eye. The front of the coat split open, and the edges were trimmed with tiny Swarovski crystals. She looked radiant as she walked down the aisle. The front of the coat opened up as it caught the air. The chiffon fluttered, and the crystals sparkled. She loved the gown so much she actually wore it again a few years later at her son's wedding.

Groom and Groomsmen

Up until now, we have been focused on getting you prepared to purchase and wear the ultimate wedding gown. Besides your own dress, your groom's attire is the most important of all! Remember, ladies: It's your fiancé's big day, too. Today's weddings are not just about the bride anymore...weddings are about *the couple*!

You will be spending the rest of your lives together, and this is the moment that you are taking that all-important step into the future with this man. He will not only be standing with you throughout your life, but today he will be standing beside you in all your photos as well. He should be just as elegant, handsome, well dressed, manicured, and accessorized as you are!

The rules that apply to formal dressing for men are stricter and more straightforward and therefore more glaring when not followed properly.

Most men act like they are not interested in fashion or even the details of their own wedding, but trust me: Men do care about how they look. As I've said before, *everyone* wants to look and feel good, and this applies to the men as well. The men at your wedding, especially your groom, shouldn't be just an afterthought!

By this time you and your fiancé should have discussed and carefully laid out your plan, look, overall theme, and colors of your wedding. You are a couple, and this wedding needs to be a reflection of *both* of you. Remember, you are telling your guests about who you are as a couple. Maybe half of your guests know you well and the other half know the groom. It is now time to tell them about who you are together.

Since I love clothes and love getting dressed up, I have my own thoughts about what your groom and the men at your wedding will be wearing.

The first questions your groom will have to ask himself regarding his attire are: Will I wear a tuxedo or suit? Will I rent or buy?

RANDY RULE #21

Your groom's attire should complement your dress in look, style, and formality.

GROOMSMEN

Your groomsmen should coordinate or complement the bridesmaids' outfits. Choose colors and hues that look good on all different groomsmen's skin tones. Make your groomsmen a checklist for a stress-free tuxedo rental. If they choose to purchase their own suit jackets, get them a swatch of fabric so everything coordinates.

Make sure your choices of dress shirt, necktie, pocket square, and any other accessories are all complementary, too.

SUIT OR TUX?

If your fiancé goes to a lot of formal occasions and he doesn't already own a nice tuxedo, I highly recommend that he buy one. If ever there were a time for him to make this purchase, this would be it! If he sticks with a classic tux, he will be able to wear it again and again and definitely get his money's worth. Consider this when choosing a tux or a suit:

- If you don't attend a lot of formal occasions, then you should consider renting.

- If you do decide to rent, keep these things in mind: The tux should be well tailored and fit like a glove! There's nothing worse than an ill-fitting tux or suit.

- Even if you are renting a tux, please splurge on a new shirt of your own. I personally wouldn't wear a shirt that had been worn by dozens of other people. A crisp white shirt will give a rented tux a fresh new look. Again, you will get good use out of it.

- If renting, I would also suggest the groom purchase his own tie. If it's a bow tie, please, guys, go for a hand-tied one and not the pretied kind. If you don't know how to tie one, now's the perfect time to learn, or ask your salesperson to tie it for you.

- If your wedding isn't ultra-formal, you can wear a beautiful suit. Personally, I prefer to see a great suit that fits you beautifully over a rented tuxedo.

- You can dress that suit up for a more formal look with a nice vest and bow tie.

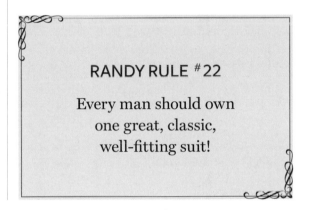

RANDY RULE #22

Every man should own
one great, classic,
well-fitting suit!

JACKET

Silhouettes aren't just for brides! Choosing the right jacket silhouette, cut, and type of lapel can drastically affect the way a man looks. Again, the correct proportion and fit are everything!

Depending on the formality and time of day of your wedding, men have a wide range of options. If you're having a daytime wedding, maybe he'll choose a morning suit. If you're getting married in the summer, he may wear a white dinner jacket instead of a standard black jacket.

The fit of a man's suit is the most important element, with the shoulder being the most important measurement in fitting a suit properly. A seam on the shoulder of the suit should sit on the tip of the shoulder. Too many times I see a man with a suit hanging off the shoulder. This creates the illusion of a little boy wearing his father's suit. It has been my experience that most men choose at least one size too large when purchasing a suit. The fabric of a suit should hug a man's body without pulling. If your groom is unsure of his size, he should see a reputable tailor to help him find his correct size. Considerations when choosing a jacket:

- You really can't go wrong with a single-breasted jacket. It generally gives men a slimmer appearance, so if you're stocky, it's especially important to choose a single-breasted suit. If you're tall and thin, you can carry off a double-breasted suit. These jackets don't look great when unbuttoned, so if you are planning on opening your jacket at your wedding, you may want to stick with a single-breasted one. However, I recommend you always keep your jacket buttoned, especially during the ceremony.

WHICH BUTTONS GET BUTTONED ON A JACKET?

Here's a simple way to remember: from the top down, if it's three buttons it's sometimes, always, never. Two buttons: always, never. One button: always.

- Morning coats are worn for formal daytime weddings. They are usually paired with gray striped trousers. However, today there are many variations available on the traditional morning suits. Be sure to choose one that fits your style.

- There are three basic lapels you should know: peaked, notched, and a shawl. All three are acceptable. The notched lapel is the least formal and the shawl is the most.

- If you decide to wear a shawl lapel, look closely at the shape of it. Does it get wider at the bottom and make your stomach look bigger or is it wider at the top tapering down, making your waist appear smaller?

- Most jackets have one of two types of vents: a center back vent, or side back vents. I prefer side back vents. If you decide to put your hands in your pockets, your jacket will hold its shape better.

- Formal tuxedo jackets sometimes don't come with vents.

- Tails are another option on a tuxedo jacket and are usually reserved for formal evening weddings.

- Look closely at the length of your jacket. Is it very long, making your legs look short? The general rule is that the length of the jacket should be just below the fingers at arm's length, but today many designers are producing a shorter silhouette. As with dresses, the groom should always *try it on.*

TROUSERS AND PANTS

Whether you are wearing tux pants with a satin or grosgrain stripe down the side, or suit pants, they should be well tailored. Consider the following when choosing pants:

• Pants should have a flat front. No pleated pants, please! They will just add bulk and look dated.

• The correct length of your pants is important. Pants should rest at the waist and be long enough for a slight break before the bottom rests on the top of your shoe. Pants that are too long look sloppy, and ones that are too short look like you should be digging for clams.

• The width of the pant leg can also play a part in the balance of the suit. Be sure that the fit is consistent.

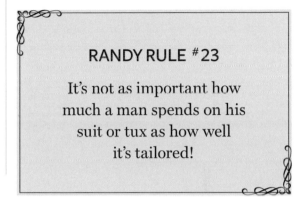

RANDY RULE #23

It's not as important how much a man spends on his suit or tux as how well it's tailored!

IF THE SUIT DOESN'T FIT

I remember the time I went to a friend's wedding. The groom had decided to rent his tuxedo from a formal-wear shop. It was a destination wedding, Iowa actually, and the shop was going to be closed by the time he arrived in town. He asked his best man to pick up the tux for him and bring it to the hotel where he would be staying.

He had been measured at one of the shop's other locations where he lived, and they called in his measurements for him. Well, my friend is very tall and very thin. He stands about six-foot-six and weighs about 160 pounds. To get a tux long enough

to accommodate his height, they selected one that was about six sizes too big. The groom called me to his room to look at it and see if I had any suggestions. Well, it looked like he was wearing his daddy's tuxedo jacket, it was so huge on him! I couldn't let him walk down the aisle like that. After careful inspection, I decided to take matters in my own hands and see if I could tailor it to fit him. I took his jacket and brought it to my hotel room. I then went to Walmart and bought a sewing machine, pins, scissors, a seam ripper, and black thread. I spent the entire night opening up the seams of the

lining and the jacket and tailoring it for him. By the time I had finished, the jacket fit like a glove and he looked as handsome as ever!

I spent the day after the wedding taking out all the seams I had sewn up returning the jacket to its original state. And although it was not how I imagined I would be spending my weekend, it was completely worth it, watching my friend walking down the aisle happy and handsome! Lesson learned: Make sure the groom's tux or suit fits *before* the wedding!

SHIRT

You can go more formal with a tux shirt or more casual with a dress shirt. Again, the most important thing is that it fits properly!

A baggy shirt will just add bulk, and the extra fabric can bunch up in the back and show through your jacket. Unless you are wearing a colored shirt, and even if your bride is wearing an off-white gown—which it will most likely be if it's silk—you should always wear a white shirt, not ivory or off-white. An off-white shirt will look like it needs to be laundered. It should be clean, fresh, and white. Considerations when choosing a shirt:

- I suggest having your shirt custom-made, or tailored if you are buying a premade one. This will ensure it fits properly.

- There are three basic collars to tux shirts: wing tip, spread, and mandarin. I prefer a spread collar.

- A dress shirt can have a spread collar, a button-down, or a mandarin. I suggest a plain spread collar.

- When it comes down to the cuffs, I prefer French cuffs. This allows you to wear a gorgeous set of cuff links. A man wearing a tux should *always* wear French cuffs.

- As a general rule, your cuff should be a quarter inch longer than your jacket sleeve for a less formal look and half an inch longer for a more formal look.

- Shirt cuffs should not ride up when you stretch your arms.

Unless you are wearing a colored shirt, and even if your bride is wearing an off-white gown…you should always wear a white shirt, not ivory or off-white.

ACCESSORIES

A man's suit or tuxedo very seldom changes from season to season. As a matter of fact, suits and tuxedos for the most part have looked almost exactly the same for decades. Where a man can really show his personal style is in his accessories: A sleek watch, a sparkling pair of diamond cuff links, a luxurious silk tie, or socks in a bright color or unusual pattern give a man the opportunity to show his individuality. Just like the bride's accessories, a man's accessories can either elevate or depreciate his look. He needs to choose them wisely. Scuffed shoes or a worn belt can really ruin a man's look. Remember, ladies, your groom will be standing beside you in almost every photo, and he needs to look his best, too. The right accessories will help him achieve this goal. Here are a list of accessories he may consider and my personal thoughts concerning them:

BELT

- If your pants have loops, you should wear a belt.
- Your belt should be in good condition and match your shoes.

BOUTONNIERE

- Set yourself apart from your groomsmen with a slightly different boutonniere.
- Try a unique boutonniere made with herbs, lavender, grains of wheat, or berries.

CUFF LINKS

- Cuff links are a great way to add some sparkle to your wardrobe.
- This is a great time to invest in a nice pair, or maybe your fiancée will buy you some.

CUMMERBUND

- A cummerbund is a large band of pleated fabric worn around the waist instead of a vest. (Note: The pleats are worn folded up.) If given the choice, go with a vest or go without.

POCKET SQUARE

- There are many different ways to fold and wear pocket squares. Whichever way you choose, you should keep in mind that it needs to be in proportion with your tie and boutonniere.
- Pocket squares can be simple and white or in colors that coordinate with the bridal party.
- The groom may choose a square that is different from his groomsmen to set him apart. I think a nice hand-rolled edge looks much finer and more elegant than a machine-stitched hem on a pocket square.

SHOES

- You can tell a lot about a man by his shoes. Invest in a good pair.
- If you're wearing a tuxedo, go for black patent leather. (If they need a shine, try glass cleaner.)
- If you wear shoes from your closet, take the time and effort to get a professional shine.
- If you are thinking about wearing tennis shoes with your suit or tux, think again. Don't!
- *Never* wear flip-flops. If you are getting married on the beach and are going for a more casual look, I suggest an elegant pair of sandals or a great pedicure with buffed toenails.

SOCKS

- Most men match their socks with their pants.
- Thinner socks are considered more formal. Thicker ones are more casual.
- Make sure your socks are long enough to cover your calves when you cross your legs.
- Today men are finding that colorful socks can be a great place to add some pizzazz and personality to your outfit. They should coordinate with your tie and pocket square. (As most of you know, I *love* to wear colored, striped, and patterned socks! I coordinate them with my tie and pocket square.)

STUD SET

- These usually come in a set of four and are used instead of buttons on a formal shirt.

TIE

- Whether you choose to wear a long tie, bow tie, or ascot, it should hold true to your look and the theme of the wedding.

- Bow ties are considered more formal and can set your groom apart from the groomsmen if they are wearing long ties.

- White is considered most formal. (Some brides order extra fabric from their gown and have their groom's tie custom-made.) Look at the size of your bow tie. Is it in proportion to your face and body? A huge bow tie will look silly if you have a smaller head and body, and vice versa.

- I would never wear a pretied bow tie. Come on, guys!

- Some men prefer to wear long ties with a tuxedo for a less stuffy look and bow ties with suits to make them look more formal.

- The size of your knot and width of your tie should be in proportion with your body and the lapel of your suit. For example: A slim tie goes well with a slim suit with a narrow lapel.

- Ascots are usually reserved for formal daytime weddings and worn with cutaway jackets and striped gray trousers.

- And unless you're getting married on a dude ranch, no bolos, please!

VEST

- Also known as waistcoats, these are a good way to personalize your suit.

- White vests are the most formal.

- You may also want to choose a color or pattern in the vest that complements what your wedding party is wearing. However, I would avoid trendy patterned vests that will look dated soon after the wedding.

- The right vest can help slim a large waist.

WATCH

- Wear an elegant watch. A slim silhouette with a black leather or croc band is considered more formal than a metal band.

For all of your men, the same rules apply:
Silhouette, proportion, and good tailoring are everything!
And again, accessories will either elevate or depreciate a man's
attire. Think about it. One bad accessory, like scruffy shoes
or a worn belt, will ruin the entire look!

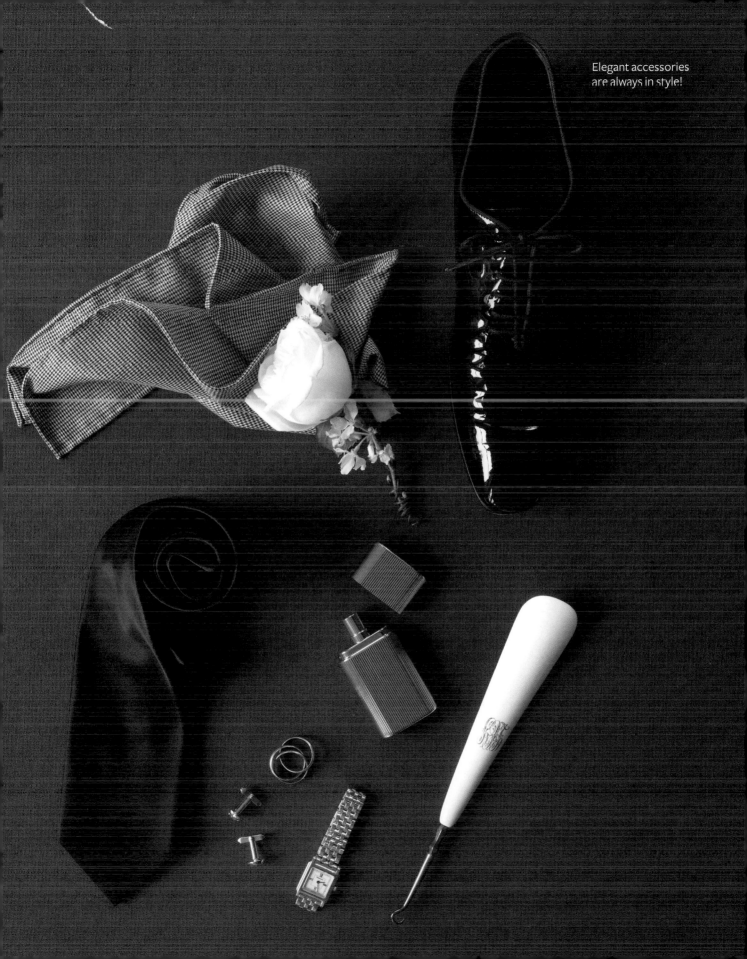

Elegant accessories
are always in style!

3–4 MONTHS BEFORE

- Decide what you and your groomsmen will wear.
- Shop for your tuxedo, suit, or other outfit.
- Make rental reservations.

1 MONTH BEFORE

- Make sure alterations are finished on your tux or suit, and make a final fitting appointment if necessary. Again, your suit or tux *must* fit properly or it will look inexpensive!

1 WEEK BEFORE

- Get a haircut.
- Write and practice saying your vows.

1–3 DAYS BEFORE

- Get your nails manicured and buffed! No polish. Remember: Everyone will be looking at your hands when you slide the ring on your bride's finger.
- Memorize your vows. You want to make sure you sound eloquent when delivering those special words.
- If you're renting or buying, double-check and put your entire outfit together to make sure you have everything. I recommend doing this before your bachelor party! Make sure everything is included, pressed, and in the correct size: jacket, trousers, shirt, tie, pocket square, vest or cummerbund, cuff links, studs, belt, suspenders, socks, and shoes.

24 HOURS BEFORE

If you will be dressing somewhere other than at home, pack up your outfit and grooming products today. Here's a checklist:

- Coat or jacket
- Trousers
- Dress shirt
- Tie
- Pocket square
- Cummerbund or vest
- Belt or suspenders
- Cuff links and studs
- Watch
- Undershirt
- Underwear
- Socks
- Shoes
- Lint brush
- Toiletries
- Wedding rings!
- Instant polish for shoes

THE DAY OF

- Get a nice close shave. Be sure to start dressing early, and allow extra time for tying your tie!
- Schedule extra time throughout your wedding day to share quiet moments with each other. Remember that today is not just about the bride, but also about the two of you as a couple. It's about sharing life together, loving each other unconditionally, and growing with each other through the seasons of your lives.

Randy's Recap

GUIDE YOUR BRIDAL PARTY TO SELECT OUTFITS THAT COMPLEMENT
THE OVERALL LOOK AND STORY OF YOUR WEDDING

·

ORDER ATTENDANTS' ATTIRE AT LEAST FOUR TO SIX MONTHS
BEFORE YOUR WEDDING DATE

·

THE MOTHERS OF THE BRIDE AND GROOM SHOULD START SHOPPING
FOR THEIR DRESSES AFTER THE BRIDE CHOOSES HER GOWN
AND BRIDESMAIDS' COLORS

·

THE MOTHERS OF THE BRIDE'S AND GROOM'S DRESSES SHOULD
MATCH IN STYLE AND FORMALITY

·

DON'T FORGET YOUR GROOM! HE SHOULD BE AS ELEGANTLY DRESSED
AND ACCESSORIZED AS YOU ARE IN STYLE AND FORMALITY

·

YOUR GROOM AND GROOMSMEN SHOULD SHOP FOR THEIR SUITS OR
TUXEDOS AT LEAST THREE TO FOUR MONTHS BEFORE THE WEDDING

·

FOR A MAN'S SUIT OR TUX, SILHOUETTE, PROPORTION,
AND GOOD TAILORING ARE IMPERATIVE!

CRYSTAL AND JEFF'S *Story*

Hometown	Boston, Massachusetts
Wedding Date	May 8
Location	Viansa Vineyard, Sonoma, California
Wedding Guests	80
Dress Designer	Lazaro

Crystal and Jeff originally wanted to marry in Tuscany, but had friends who couldn't travel abroad, so they decided to have their destination wedding at a winery in Sonoma, California. Although they were marrying in a wine cave, Crystal still wanted a gown that reflected the Old World feeling of Tuscany.

I met Crystal in the salon on a very busy Saturday. She had driven all the way from Boston to try on a specific Lazaro gown that was on our website. Unfortunately, the gown could not be found! I remembered seeing the gown earlier that week. It had been torn and was filed away in the back getting ready to be shipped back to the designer to be replaced. When Crystal tried on the tattered sample I brought her, she realized it wasn't the one. I asked her to tell me about her wedding and how she wanted to look. Once she gave me a brief description, I immediately thought of another Lazaro gown that had the same silhouette she was looking for, but was exquisitely beaded. The beading on this gown was unique and done in an ornate scroll-like pattern that reminded me of the wrought-iron gates of Tuscany. It had pearlized beads, hand-embroidered thread flowers, Swarovski crystals, and insets of delicately beaded Chantilly lace. When she put on the dress, she got teary-eyed. We knew this was her gown. Crystal recalled, "Even though the gown had a feeling of Tuscany, it was also perfect for our wedding in the organic setting of California vineyards.

"My best accessory for the wedding was definitely having Jeff on my arm! Jeff was the first groom to ever wear a Randy Fenoli tuxedo. The tuxedo lining had Randy's signature red-and-pink-striped piping. Even better, as a nod to Randy, Jeff sported socks accented in hot pink. Randy made us feel like this was so much more than just a dress that we were buying. We were celebrating our story and sharing this experience. He recognized how much Jeff and I had planned this event together. The whole wedding was *our* vision. Teamwork!"

Crystal's gown embodied the look of Tuscany, but worked perfectly for her vineyard wedding.

CHAPTER TEN

YOUR *B*IG DAY

You've dreamed about this day a million times.
Don't rush through it.

Congratulations, beautiful, you've made it! This is your big day!

Today is one of the most monumental days in your life, and you're almost ready to walk down that aisle. Before you do, I want you to make sure everything is ready, and you are fully prepared.

It's important you get a good night's rest so that you feel fresh. It's going to be a long day and you will need your strength. Remember to eat a good breakfast, and lunch if your wedding is in the evening. Also, drink plenty of water to keep hydrated.

There are many things you can do to help make sure this day goes smoothly—from making sure that everyone in the bridal party knows how they can help, to ensuring you have everything with you that you may need. And, of course, you should remember to enjoy this day...every minute of it.

Final Preparations for the Bride

Everyone loves to be included! Make sure your wedding party knows that they are supporting characters in your story and play an important part in your big day.

To keep things running smoothly, choose something you can delegate to key people in your bridal party.

I'm not saying you should hand over the important decisions of your big day. When you share some of the day's tasks, however, you and your groom will be less overwhelmed and better able to cherish those special moments.

The most important person to help you anticipate and handle emergencies is your attendant. You need to choose one special person—most likely your maid of honor, or in some cases, man of honor—to be on hand and help you get through your wedding. Whoever gets this job must be prepared. *She is there today to help you with everything you may need.*

Be sure you choose someone who is considerate, helpful, and who can anticipate your needs. Your attendant should know how to stay calm in a crisis. She should know everyone involved with the wedding day. This means you should tell her about all the vendors responsible for your day. Program all the important phone numbers you may need into your attendant's cell phone ahead of time, just in case. Since most brides don't carry purses, your attendant should have extra cash or checks with her for anything that may come up.

> Remember that part of being empowered is being able to rely on other people.

Your attendant may also help you get dressed, and be there when it comes time to bustle your gown. These duties can be a lot for one person to handle by him- or herself, so your attendant may need to identify a support team to help.

Even more important, you should remember that part of being empowered is being able to rely on other people. No one can do everything themselves. If you are going to fully enjoy your day, you need to trust your attendant.

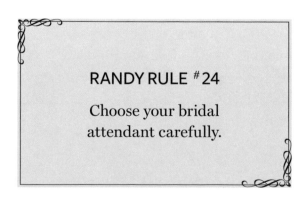

RANDY RULE #24

Choose your bridal attendant carefully.

YOUR WEDDING DAY EMERGENCY KIT

I recommend your attendant or bridesmaids assemble and be responsible for an all-purpose emergency kit. This is a collection of items for unexpected emergencies that may arise. The contents of your emergency kit should be assembled at least one week before your wedding. If you see something missing from this list—add it!

- SEWING KIT WITH THREAD to match the colors of the bride's and wedding party's dresses, plus black
- AT LEAST ONE NEEDLE AND THREAD already knotted and ready to go in all colors
- SAFETY PINS IN ASSORTED SIZES, including extra-large safety pins in case the bustle breaks
- EXTRA EARRING BACKS
- EXTRA STOCKINGS
- SUPERGLUE
- STAIN REMOVER
- DOUBLE-SIDED TAPE for quick hem fixes
- STATIC-CLING SPRAY
- CROCHET HOOK to help with buttons and loops on the wedding gown
- CLEAR NAIL POLISH (helpful for stocking runs)
- NAIL FILE
- NAIL POLISH in the bride's shade

- HAND MIRROR
- PLASTIC STRAWS for drinking without messing up lipstick
- HAIR SPRAY and other hair products
- BRUSH AND COMB
- HAIR PINS, BOBBY PINS, AND ELASTIC BANDS
- HAIR DRYER
- TISSUES
- Q-TIPS
- HANDKERCHIEFS
- LINT BRUSH
- BABY POWDER
- EYEDROPS
- CONTACT LENS SOLUTION (if you wear lenses)
- ANTACID
- MINTS
- HEADACHE MEDICINE (bring two different kinds in case someone in the bridal party is allergic)

- ALLERGY MEDICINE (If needed, nondrowsy formula)
- BAND-AIDS (not the neon kind)
- MOIST TOWELETTES
- TAMPONS AND PADS
- BOTTLES OF WATER
- CHARGED CELL PHONE
- CELL PHONE CHARGER
- CAMERA for taking candid photographs
- WRISTWATCH
- HEALTHY SNACKS
- DENTAL FLOSS
- TOOTHBRUSH, TOOTHPASTE, AND MOUTHWASH
- EXTENSION CORD
- TRAVEL STEAMER (I recommend a Rowenta travel steamer)
- HAND LOTION
- OIL-ABSORBING BLOTTING PAPERS

As a final preparation for the big day, double-check everything about your plan. Make sure you've considered all the logistics. Below are a few last-minute checks for you to ask yourself and your bridal party:

• How will your gown get to your venue? This is especially important if you are traveling to a destination wedding.

• Is there a restroom and changing room conveniently located at your wedding site? You will need a place to get ready and to perform last-minute touch-ups before you walk down the aisle.

• Is there a full-length mirror so you will be able to take one last glance at your ensemble? Have an attendant bring a handheld mirror so you can check the *back* of your hairstyle and your dress.

• Is there adequate lighting in the room or area where you will be getting dressed?

• Have you planned for some time during the wedding celebration when you and the groom will be *alone*? This is essential. Keep in mind this wedding is about the celebration and union of two people in love. Again, take time to enjoy each other.

Remember to consider the people in your bridal party and show them how appreciative you are.

One way to show your appreciation for the support of your bridesmaids, mothers of the bride and groom, and your fiancé is to give them thank-you notes or gifts. These tokens should be heartfelt, personal, and meaningful. If you decide to handwrite notes to thank your wedding party, make sure you do this in advance. You want to be able to have time during your wedding to enjoy your guests and all of the festivities.

Your big day is here. Are you ready?

Keep in mind this wedding is about the
celebration and union of two people in love…
take time to enjoy each other.

Handing Linda
her bouquet.

Walking Down the Aisle

This is the moment you've been looking forward to for a long time. It's the moment when you will walk not just down that aisle, but toward your husband, your future, and into your new life.

It may be your father, or both parents, or another significant family member standing there beside you. Or you may decide to walk down the aisle alone. Either way, remember I am right beside you to help you walk down that aisle. That's right! I've been here throughout this entire process and am not leaving you yet!

As you step into view in front of your guests, there are some important things I want you to keep in mind.

First, lower your bouquet, take a deep breath, and relax. Brides often raise their hands when they get excited, and hide themselves and their dress behind their bouquets. You want to keep your flowers low so everyone can see you and the details of your dress and your waist.

Now lift your head and look down the aisle. Do you see your family, friends, and loved ones?

Okay.

Pause.

Yes. I want you to stop.

You've dreamed about this moment a million times.

Don't rush through it. Take time to take in the sights and sounds. Look around and take in the view. You will want to remember this stroll down the aisle for the rest of your life.

As I said before, your wedding is like the Academy Awards, except you're walking down the "white" carpet. Trust me, *everyone* wants to see you and take in your beauty. *And* they want to see what you're wearing.

I'm sure you want to see them, too.

Take time to make eye contact with the people you love. It may feel like you don't have time to do this, but you do, and for your guests it's a worthwhile pause. Your family and friends took time out of their busy lives to share this occasion with you and your fiancé. They want you to know they're here with you. They've come to support you not only on this day, but throughout your life. And I'm positive they want to see your beaming face, and take in the beauty of your magnificent dress!

Wait as long as you need to wait. Don't worry. Trust me, your fiancé will wait a few more seconds at the other end of the aisle! In fact, just before you take your first step, lock eyes and meet his stare.

RANDY RULE #25

Take time to be in
the moment.

Alisa practicing
for her walk
down the aisle.

You've gone through a lot to get to this place and learned many lessons along the way. There have been ups and downs and twists and turns. I tell brides that planning a wedding is like riding a roller coaster: "You're strapped in and it has left the station. You have one of two choices. You can drop your head over the side and throw up; or you can throw your hands up in the air and enjoy the ride."

I suggest you enjoy the ride!

In my life, I've always had strong beliefs, thoughts, prayers, and sayings that have gotten me through. When I was stuck on that farm all those years ago, thinking there was no escape, I would stop sometimes, too, and take a moment to figure things out and decide where I wanted to go. I remember the moment I saw Mother's yellow dress billowing through the field. Somehow that dress offered me a light at the end of the tunnel.

Sometimes things people say can help guide us at life's most pivotal moments; moments like right now.

So let me say this: For everyone reading this book, I hope that you have gotten more than just a guide to finding your perfect dress. I want every woman to realize her own beauty and style. You deserve it. So many women have body image issues. We are all constantly reminded by magazine ads, filled with super-skinny models who have been unrealistically airbrushed, that this is our society's perception of beauty. Are we thin enough? Are we pretty enough? Is our gown expensive enough? Standing in front of a full-length mirror while shopping for your wedding gown and listening to people make comments can bring up many of these issues. I understand that. I know that some parts of this process are not easy.

That's why I will remind you again and again. Remember to love yourself and *own* your story! Stand tall and realize your beauty!

I said clothes can make you feel. Every day when I get dressed and put on clothes I love, they help me feel empowered. This is what I want your wedding dress to do for you.

I want you to feel beautiful and be empowered!

Think about the brides featured in this book. Take a closer look at their stories, their obstacles, their courage, their hope, and their triumphs. Let their stories inspire you.

Remember to love yourself and *own* your story!
Stand tall and realize your beauty!

Pam stands tall, confident, and stunning!

Pam found love in her forties. She *challenged* traditional thinking, found her inner princess, and told her story her way: with a sparkling princess gown, her children by her side, and a colorful tattoo proudly displayed across her back.

Jessica found the *courage* to be herself and own her story. She walked down the aisle wearing giant fairy wings toward her fiancé standing in his knight's armor.

Amanda stayed *strong* when everyone told her no. She didn't give up the pursuit of her dream dress and ultimately wore the Carolina Herrera gown she had her heart set on.

Shannon gave away a prize worth $3,000 to *discover* the true gown of her dreams!

Allison *realized* just how important family is in her life and wed her fiancé in the backyard of her childhood home wearing a dress that made her feel romantic and expressed her personality.

Anna had the *faith* to purchase her perfect dress before her now-husband, Geoffrey, had even proposed to her.

Alexis found her *inner strength* after a series of mishaps threatened to ruin her big day and became the "Glamour Girl" she always knew she could be.

Amy had the *conviction* to go through the process of trying on five hundred wedding gowns until she ultimately found "the one."

Crystal and Jeff *committed* to each other and combined their separate stories to become one great story. Jeff was *secure* enough in himself to sport bright pink socks on his wedding day!

Rhonda *took a risk* and tried on a ruffled gown completely out of her comfort zone that in the end revealed a romantic, softer inner self she had been hiding for so long.

At the age of sixty-two and widowed, Linda stayed *hopeful* and found love and a new life partner for the next chapter of her life.

Jessica took a huge leap of *faith* and a flight over fifteen hundred miles away from home to prove to everyone that plus-size girls are beautiful, too!

After turning fifty, Susan *overcame* insecurities with her own beauty and walked down that aisle tall, beautiful, and *empowered*!

These are their stories. What is *your* story?

We all share life's obstacles. What makes us different is how we deal with them. You can't always control what happens to you in life, but you *can* control how you react to it. You can choose to move ahead, and move to new heights.

Which brings me back to the big day and this big moment.

It's time to walk.

Your future is waiting. Everyone's eyes are on you. It's all about you and your fiancé. It's about your story, your strength, your beauty, and your power. It's all about this day. And it's all about your dress.

May you always look and feel this stunning! Good-bye, beautiful!

Love,

RANDY'S RULES

RANDY RULE #1
For every rule, there is an exception.

RANDY RULE #2
Establish *your* story!

RANDY RULE #3
Establish a budget.

RANDY RULE #4
How you wear your dress is more important than how much you spend on it.

RANDY RULE #5
You can always purchase a cheaper dress, but in the end it will be only the price that you love.

RANDY RULE #6
Don't wait until the last minute to shop for your wedding gown!

RANDY RULE #7
Your body is not defined by a list of shapes.

RANDY RULE #8
Never purchase a wedding dress without trying it on first.

RANDY RULE #9
It's not about size; it's about silhouette and proportion.

RANDY RULE #10
Everyone has an opinion. Make sure yours is heard.

RANDY RULE #11
You should *always* purchase the gown that makes you feel the most beautiful!

RANDY RULE #12
When making changes to a dress, always get the details in writing.

RANDY RULE #13
Without a veil, you're just a pretty girl in a white dress.

RANDY RULE #14
Accessories will either elevate or depreciate your look. Choose them wisely!

RANDY RULE #15
When in doubt, less jewelry is more.

RANDY RULE #16
Your bouquet should not be bigger than your head.

RANDY RULE #17
Do not skimp on alterations! Your gown must fit properly!

RANDY RULE #18
I don't believe in Bridezillas!

RANDY RULE #19
When selecting bridesmaids' dresses, ask yourself, "Would I be happy wearing this?"

RANDY RULE #20
Encourage everyone in your bridal party to dress elegantly and to feel confident.

RANDY RULE #21
Your groom's attire should complement your dress in look, style, and formality.

RANDY RULE #22
Every man should own one great, classic, well-fitting suit!

RANDY RULE #23
It's not as important how much a man spends on his suit or tux as how well it's tailored!

RANDY RULE #24
Choose your bridal attendant carefully.

RANDY RULE #25
Take time to be in the moment.

RANDY'S BRIDAL BASICS

Although I do not want to overwhelm you with a long list of bridal terms, I do want to make sure this book offers you things you need to know to help prepare you for your big day. Here is a list of some basic terms that will help you with your selection of the perfect dress.

A

A-line silhouette: This silhouette refers to a shape of gown that resembles the letter A. The gown can be anything from a slim to a full A-line.

Alençon lace: The most popular choice for wedding dresses, this lace originated in the town of Alençon, France. It usually features flowers or swirls that are outlined with a heavy silky cording on a net background. Can be used as an allover fabric or for appliqués.

Appliqué: Decorative pieces of fabric, embroidery, or lace that are sewn or attached onto a gown.

B

Ball gown silhouette: A gown with a dramatically full skirt that typically has a natural or dropped waist.

Ballerina-length skirt: A full skirt that falls just above the ankle.

Basque waist: A dropped waist that has a V shape.

Bateau neckline: A neckline that is open from shoulder to shoulder and follows the line of your collarbone. Also known as a boat or Sabrina neckline.

Beading: The decorative application of beads, gemstones, crystals, glass, or similar materials that are sewn onto fabric.

Blusher: A veil that is usually worn forward to cover a bride's face and then lifted during the ceremony.

Bolero jacket: A short jacket, with or without sleeves, that falls no longer than the waistline. Of Spanish origin, this type of jacket is worn open in front.

Brocade: A thick, heavy, jacquard-woven fabric with a raised design, most often featuring a floral pattern.

Brooch: A decorative piece of jewelry that is usually attached to a garment with a pin.

Bubble skirt: A top skirt that is gathered and then attached to the lining at the hemline to create a bubble effect.

Bubble veil: A veil that has all of its edges gathered together and typically attached to a comb to create a bubble.

Bustier: A formfitting and often strapless top or undergarment. Its primary purpose is to enhance the bust by tightening around the upper midriff in order to push the breasts up and gently shape the waist.

Bustle: A method by which the train on a gown is picked up and secured to make the skirt floor-length.

C

Cage veil: A very short veil that typically attaches to a comb. It usually comes forward and covers half or all of the face and is generally made of wide French netting or tulle.

Cap sleeve: This short, fitted sleeve barely covers the shoulder and top of the arm.

Capelet: A small cape that is worn over the shoulders.

Cathedral train: A long train that extends three or more feet on the floor.

Cathedral veil: A veil that measures nine feet long or that falls twelve to eighteen inches past a cathedral train.

Chantilly lace: A very delicate, lightweight lace that originated in Chantilly, France, and is usually made of a blend of rayon, cotton, or nylon. It has a fine mesh, and often features a floral design. It is flat, unlike re-embroidered Alençon lace, which has raised cording.

Chapel train: A mid-length train that extends about two to three feet on the floor.

Chapel veil: A veil that typically measures twelve to eighteen inches past a chapel train.

Charmeuse: A shiny, lightweight fabric with a very soft drape.

Chiffon: A delicate, transparent, and sheer fabric made from silk or polyester. It is often layered, gathered, draped, or used for sheer sleeves.

Circular skirt: A skirt that makes a complete circle at the hemline.

Corset: A formfitting, usually strapless bodice with boning, styled in the fashion of a ladies undergarment of the same name.

Crepe: A medium-weight fabric with a matte, slightly coarse finish.

Crown: A circular headpiece that sits on the crown of the head.

D

Décolletage: Generally refers to an open neckline.

Dropped waistline: This waistline falls below your natural waist. It can be shaped straight across, into a V-shape called a Basque waist, or as a scoop or square, or even inverted.

Dupioni: A fabric, usually made of silk, that is thicker and coarser than shantung.

E

Elbow-length veil: A veil that ends at the elbow.

Embroidery: Decorative needlework or stitching on fabric done with thread or yarn by hand or machine.

Empire waistline: A high waistline that falls above the natural waist, usually right under the bust.

F

Faille: A medium-weight fabric that can be slightly stiff and has a low luster. Its main characteristic is its tiny raised ribs that are similar to, but finer than, a grosgrain ribbon.

Fingertip veil: This veil ends at or just past the fingertips.

Fit-to-flare silhouette: Also known as a modified A-line, this silhouette is fitted to the upper thighs and gently flares out at the bottom of the dress. (It's fitted more closely than an A-line, but flares out more gently than a trumpet.)

Floor-length: Describes a gown that falls at or just above the floor and has no train.

Fold-over veil: A veil made from one piece of material, usually tulle, which is folded over. It can be any length, and the top layer can be pulled over the face and used as a blusher.

French bustle: A bustle that is created by lifting the train at the middle of the skirt and pulling it under the back of the skirt, where it is then attached with ribbons or buttons and loops.

G

Gazar: A loosely woven fabric with a low luster. It looks like a thick, dense organza with a crisp finish, and is very buoyant.

Godet: A triangular piece of fabric

that is inserted into a seam of a skirt to give fullness or flare.

Guipure lace: A heavy, raised lace with an open background, usually with large floral leafy patterns that are joined by threads. Guipure lace can be used as an allover fabric or for appliqués.

H

Halter neckline: The neckline created by a sleeveless top that has two straps which connect at the back of the neck. It can be square, rounded, or V-shaped.

Hem bustle: A bustle that is created by bringing up the hem of a train and attaching it underneath a skirt using ribbons or buttons and loops. The train is set long enough to make the back of the gown floor-length and bunched to create a "bubble hem" effect.

I

Illusion (also known as Tulle): A delicate and very sheer fine netting or mesh fabric made from nylon, silk, or rayon. It is typically used for veils.

J

Jewel neckline: A round neckline that rests at the base of the neck.

Juliet cap: A small cap that is often decorated with lace, pearls, or beads and that hugs the back of the head.

K

Keyhole neckline: An opening at the front or back of a bodice. It can be shaped in a circle, oval, or teardrop.

L

Lace: An ornamental openwork patterned fabric. It generally has a floral motif.

M

Mermaid silhouette: A fitted gown that has a seam above the knee with a skirt attached that flares out very full to the bottom hem.

Mikado: A heavier weight twill weave fabric with a medium luster.

Moire: A heavy taffeta with a wavy design.

N

Natural waistline: A waistline that falls right at your natural waist.

O

Off-the-shoulder neckline: The fabric sits off the shoulders and wraps around your arms. The neckline can be a V, scoop, square, or sweetheart.

On-the-shoulder neckline: The fabric rests on the shoulders. It can be a V, scoop, square, or sweetheart shape.

Organdy: A lightweight, stiff, and transparent plain-weave fabric.

Organza: A very lightweight, plain-weave, sheer, and crisp fabric. It can be made from silk, rayon, polyester, or nylon.

P

Peplum: A short overskirt or flounce attached at the waist of a garment.

Petticoat: An underskirt, usually made of stiff netting or tulle, that is used to reinforce the silhouette of the skirt.

Point d'esprit lace: A lightweight lace with dots woven on a mesh background.

Princess seams: Vertical seams in the front or back of a garment that shape the bust and waist.

S

Sabrina neckline: Also called a bateau or boat neckline. The name was coined from the movie *Sabrina* that starred Audrey Hepburn.

Satin: A fabric that is densely woven and typically lustrous on one side and dull on the other. It can be made of acetate, polyester, or silk. It comes in different weights, with duchesse satin being the heaviest.

Satin-organza: A medium- to lightweight fabric with a sheen on the front and matte finish on the back.

Schiffli lace: A type of machine-made lace created by embroidering a pattern on a fabric that has been chemically treated to disintegrate after the pattern has been created.

Scoop neckline: A rounded, low, U-shaped front or back neckline that dips from the shoulders.

Sequins: Shiny, sometimes iridescent, highly reflective or matte plastic discs sewn onto fabric to add sparkle or ornamentation.

Shantung: A medium-weight fabric that is semi-lustrous and usually made of raw silk. Its main characteristic is its tiny slubs of raw silk running through it. It was originally woven in Shantung, China.

Shawl: A rectangular or oblong garment or piece of fabric, used as a covering for the shoulders or carried on the arm.

Sheath: A slim gown that hugs the body and has a straight shape.

Shrug: A small jacket that falls above the waistline, usually shorter than a bolero.

Silhouette: The shape of a garment or dress.

Silk: A soft and fine fiber that comes from the cocoons of the larvae of silkworms and is woven into fabrics.

Stole: A wide scarf, sometimes made of an expensive fabric or fur, that is worn about the shoulders.

Strapless neckline: Refers to the neckline created by a bodice that has no sleeves. It can be shaped straight across, dipped, sweetheart, or even raised.

Sweep train: The shortest train, a sweep train extends a foot or less from where the hem hits the floor.

Sweetheart-front neckline: This open neckline is shaped like the top of a heart across the bust.

T

Taffeta: A thin, crisp, lightweight fabric with a very fine rib. It is tightly woven and looks the same on both sides.

Tea length: A skirt with a hemline that falls several inches above the ankles.

Tiara: An ornamental half-crown that sits on the head, often made of crystals, pearls, rhinestones, or diamonds.

Tip-of-the-shoulder neckline: A neckline created when the top of the bodice rests at the tip of your shoulders. It can have different shapes, such as V, scoop, square, or sweetheart.

Traditional bustle: A bustle that is created when the fabric from a train is pulled up and over the skirt

and attached with buttons and loops or hooks and eyes.

Train: The longer fabric that extends from the back of a skirt to trail on the floor.

Trumpet silhouette: A fitted gown that is similar to a mermaid, but flares out more gently to the bottom hem. Its gentle flare is usually made with princess seams instead of a seam above the knee.

Tulle: A delicate and very sheer fine netting or mesh fabric made from nylon, silk, or rayon. It is typically used for veils and can also be used for skirts. It's often referred to as illusion.

V

V-neckline: A front or back neckline shaped like the letter V. It can be a shallow or very deep V.

Velvet: A plush, thick fabric that can be made of silk, polyester, rayon, or cotton, and that has a soft, thick, short pile.

W

Waltz-length veil: A veil that stops at the floor and is usually worn with a floor-length gown.

Watteau train: A train that falls from the shoulders.

Wrap: Any garment or fabric that wraps around the shoulders or body.

ACKNOWLEDGMENTS

My sincerest appreciation to everyone who helped make my book a beautiful reality.

To my incredible book agent Jill Cohen. You opened the door for me to become an author and guided me through the process.

Heartfelt appreciation and thanks to my amazing editor, Karen Murgolo, who believed in my book, who held my hand, and who worked so hard and patiently with me throughout the entire process.

To Pippa White, for your time and invaluable help with this project.

My sincerest thanks to the entire publishing team at Hachette, including: Matthew Ballast in publicity, Peggy Boelke and Nicole Bond in subsidiary rights, Tareth Mitch in managing editorial, copy editor Laura Jorstad, art director Anne Twomey, and Suzanne Albert and Carol Meadows in special sales.

To the absolutely *brilliant* Eric Hoffman and Tracy Engelhardtsen for their creative direction and for making the pages of my book come together and come to life. I am eternally grateful to you!

To my *genious* photographer François Dischinger! The infectious energy and extreme talent you brought on set truly shows in the gorgeous photographs you've provided throughout this book. Thanks to Keith Ketwaroo, whose retouching was perfect, and to the rest of your talented crew, including Jeremy Schmidt.

For the *stunning* video footage: Jonathan Rubin, Dan King, and Collin Emley.

A very special thanks to my very organized and life-saving production assistant: Michael Landry.

To my manager, Dennis Johnson, who puts up with me, believes in me, and does the most amazing job of making some sense out of my crazy life!

To Laura Dower, who laid out the framework of the book and helped me find my voice.

I couldn't have done this book without my absolutely incredible team of makeup artists, hair stylists, florists, pressers, and people who helped me photograph twenty-eight real brides in just three days!

Gorgeous hair by: Ramona Azcona-Solages, **Celinet Mendez, Jeanne Carosone, Jacqueline Cookson, a**nd Gad Cohen.

Flawless makeup by: Christina Amador, Monica Boyd-Lester, Sir John B, and Lisa Juarez-Russo.

Crystal tattoo artistry by: Lisa Juarez-Russo.

Exquisite bouquets by: Florisity, Stellar Style Events, and Kurt Rausch for Flowers, LLC.

Boutonniere by: Florisity.

Beautiful tuxedo and menswear accessories graciously provided by: Kleinfeld Men and Eric Hoffman.

Elegant French laces provided by: Marilyn and Ken at Gelmor Trading Co.

Luxurious fabrics provided by: Michael at Super Textiles.

Thank you to my invaluable set assistants: Myrna Plaisir Daramy, Lauren Deitrich, Jillian Totaro, Ingrid Wenzler, Milly Ali, Melissa Guichardo, Megan Saverine, and Lisa Juarez-Russo.

My pressers: Mary Cheong, Marguerite ImTanios, Gehan Waheeh, Nora Ulloa, Helen Ledakis, and Iveline Lan.

Thanks to those listed below, and to the many who I have surely left out. You have all come into my life and made it even richer. From the bottom of my heart, I love you and thank you all for helping me through this journey I call life.

My mother, who told me I could do anything.

Michael Landry, for loving me unconditionally and

making my life worth living.

Linda Fenoli, who made me feel loved.

Jim Fenoli, who rescued me from my father.

Marilyn Fenoli, for being my surrogate mother, my sister, and my best friend.

Joe Llaine Long, who saw artistic talent and pushed me to achieve.

Nell Grigg, who put me in front of the class and made me speak.

Mike Tinerello, who gave me the book *The Magic of Thinking Big*.

Mitch Kinchen, for wearing turquoise pumps and telling me to do it for myself.

Jeff Plaisance, for that memorable ride on Florida Boulevard and peanut butter and jelly sandwiches.

Cory Wise, for Biloxi Beach and great times on Carolyn Sue Drive.

Chris Stroud, for all those mad drives to the airport.

David Lowman, for holding my photos in Indianapolis and for holding our friendship even closer.

Norman Jones, for gracing me with a crown and one of the best years and memories of my life.

Linda Tain, who took me under her wing and guided me as if I were her child.

Jo Marie Di Iorio, who taught me the love and art of draping.

Paul and Vivian Diamond, who saw talent in me, called me on a pay phone, and gave me the opportunity of my lifetime.

Michelle Nagy-Gauss, my dear friend, for those Second Avenue parties, Mustang convertibles, Mexico, and waiting for me in hotel lobbies.

Michael Scully, for that first dance at the Roxy and for loving me for just being me.

Dovi Alpert, who always looks after Mr. Fenolowitz.

Magnolia Honorio, who was always my friend and brought me a sewing machine when I was in need.

Dr. Gerald Leichman, for making me a part of your family and for making sure my glass was always full.

Lizzy Romanski, for wild times in New Orleans and those crazy videos at the Hudson Hotel.

Rebecca Grinnals, for those insane nights at the St. Regis Hotel, fun times at Disney World, Grand Cayman, and many other special moments, I love you, my dear friend.

Rochelle La Montagne-Kwasnowski, I kept the wrinkles out of your wedding dress, you keep our friendship in my heart, and you're always there to give me love and great advice.

Tyler Evertson, for always keeping me in trouble!

Ty and Nanny Yeh, for seeing talent in me, and giving me two chances.

Dr. Cindy Ashkins, for helping me through those rough times after Katrina.

Jonathan Rubin, for giving me great photos, videos, and friendship.

Ronnie Rothstein and Mara Urshel, for bringing me back into bridal, the passion of my life.

My Kleinfeld family, to the consultants, stock girls, and everyone who makes working there a pleasure.

My TLC/Discovery family, for believing in me and giving me some of the most incredible opportunities of my life!

My family at Half Yard, who films me, lights me beautifully, edits me ingeniously, and who share special friendships with me.

I especially want to thank the beautiful and courageous models that grace these pages. They have given their hearts, bared their souls, and put their trust in me to tell their stories.

FASHION CREDITS

ALEXIS
Pages 9, 81, 93, 101, 117, 150, 165
Dress: *Pnina Tornai* Jewelry: *her own*
Evening Bag: *Maria Elena* Shoes:
Christian Louboutin Hair: *Gad Cohen*
Makeup: *Christina Amador*

ALISA
Pages 22, 90, 211
Dress: *Reem Acra* Veil: *Erin Cole*
Jewelry: *Bashinski* Shoes: *Kate Spade*
Hair: *Jeanne Carosone* Makeup:
Christina Amador

ALLISON
Pages ii, 33, 106, 204
Dress: *Christos* Jewelry: *Heirloom*
Shoes: *J. Crew* Headpiece: *Lori
London* Hair: *Ramona Azcona*
Makeup: *Christina Amador*

AMANDA
Pages 42, 72, 79, 164
Dress: *Carolina Herrera* Veil: *Vera
Wang* Jewelry: *Otto Jakob* Shoes:
Valentino Hair: *Gad Cohen* Makeup:
Christina Amador

AMY
Pages 47, 148, 169
Dress: *Monique Lhuillier* Jewelry:
*earrings—Van Cleef & Arpels;
necklace—Edwardian vintage* Shoes:
Stuart Weitzman Hair: *Ramona
Azcona* Makeup: *Christina Amador*
Flowers: *Stellar Style Events*

ANNA
Pages 61, 70, 102
Dress: *Monique Lhuillier* Veil:
Kleinfeld Bridal Jewelry: *Richard
Wasserman Designs* Shoes: *Christian
Louboutin* Hair: *Ramona Azcona*
Makeup: *Monica Boyd-Lester*

BREANNE
Pages vi, 110, 153
Dress: *Carolina Herrera* Headpiece:
Ellen Christine Shoes: *Christian
Louboutin* Hair: *Jeanne Carosone*
Makeup: *Sir John B* Flowers: *Florisity*

BRIANNE
Pages 9, 40, 58, 92, 101, 165
Dress: *Lazaro* Jewelry: *Elements*
Shoes: *Martinez Valero* Headpiece:
Malis Henderson Hair: *Gad Cohen*
Makeup: *Christina Amador*
Flowers: *Stellar Style Events*

BROOKE
Pages 47, 52, 98
Dress: *Badgley Mischka* Veil:
Kleinfeld Bridal Jewelry: *vintage*
Headpiece: *Maria Elena* Shoes:
Coloriffics Hair: *Jeanne Carosone*
Makeup: *Monica Boyd-Lester*

CHARMAINE
Pages 10, 45, 153, 166
Dress: *Pnina Tornai* Jewelry:
*earrings and necklace—Nadri;
bracelet—Crislu* Shoes: *Gucci* Hair:
Ramona Azcona Makeup: *Christina
Amador* Flowers: *Kurt Rausch for
Flowers*

CRYSTAL
Pages 33, 144, 174, 202
Dress: *Lazaro* Veil: *Lazaro* Jewelry:
her own Shoes: *Manolo Blahnik*
Hair: *Ramona Azcona* Makeup:
Christina Amador

JENNIFER
Pages viii, 33, 56, 113, 165
Dress: *Rivini* Jewelry: *Nyjole Jewellery*
Shoes: *Ralph Lauren* Hair: *Celinet*

Mendez Makeup: *Monica Boyd-Lester*
Flowers: *Kurt Rausch for Flowers*

JESSICA C.
Pages 58, 87, 92, 131, 184
Dress: *Pnina Tornai* Veil: *Homa*
Jewelry: *earrings—Nadri; bracelet —
Homa* Headpiece: *Homa* Hair:
Ramona Azcona Makeup: *Monica
Boyd-Lester* Flowers: *Florisity*

JESSICA R.
Pages 9, 13, 37, 47, 60, 92
Dress: *Lazaro* Veil: *Christina
Garcia* Jewelry: *Maria Horn* Shoes:
Guisseppe Zanotti Hair: *Gad Cohen*
Makeup: *Christina Amador*

JESSICA S.
Pages 13, 105
Dress: *Pnina Tornai* Shoes: *Joey O*
Headpiece: *Maria Elena* Wings: *Up
from the Ashes* Hair: *Ramona Azcona*
Makeup: *Christina Amador*

JESSICA W.
Pages 88, 96, 170
Dress: *Rivini* Shoes: *Stuart
Weitzman* Jewelry: *Hoffman
Diamond Company* Hair: *Celinet
Mendez* Makeup: *Christina Amador*
Flowers: *Florisity*

JILL
Pages 114, 158, 165, 227
Dress: *Romona Keveza* Silk Organza
Coat: *Romona Keveza* Jewelry:
*brooch—Thomas Knoell; earrings—
her own* Shoes: *Stuart Weitzman*
Hair: *Celinet Mendez* Makeup:
Monica Boyd-Lester

YEKATERINA "KATE"
Pages 13, 58, 109

Dress: *Claire Pettibone* Veil: *custom* Jewelry: *vintage* Shoes: *Cole Haan* Hair: *Ramona Azcona* Makeup: *Sir John B*

KELLY
Pages 74, 84, 153
Dress: *Pnina Tornai* Veil: *Kleinfeld Bridal* Jewelry: *Thomas Knoell, her own* Headpiece: *Thomas Knoell* Shoes: *Enzo Angiolini* Hair: *Ramona Azcona* Makeup: *Christina Amador* Flowers: *Stellar Style Events*

LINDA
Pages 9, 16, 93, 122, 208
Dress: *Elizabeth Fillmore* Veil: *Kleinfeld Bridal* Jewelry: *De Picciotto/ Renee Pawele* Shoes: *Grace* Hair: *Celinet Mendez* Makeup: *Monica Boyd-Lester* Flowers: *Florisity*

LINIQUE
Pages 159, 181
Dress: *Alita Graham* Veil: *David's Bridal* Jewelry: *vintage* Shoes: *Badgley Mischka* Hair: *Ramona Azcona* Makeup: *Monica Boyd-Lester*

PAM H-F
Pages 20, 47, 212
Dress: *Eve of Milady* Veil: *Bel-Aire* Jewelry: *Thomas Knoell* Shoes: *Jimmy Choo* Hair: *Jeanne Carosone* Makeup: *Sir John B* Flowers: *Kurt Rausch for Flowers*

PAMELA W.
Pages 93, 132
Dress: *Romona Keveza* Veil: *Kleinfeld Bridal* Jewelry: *Thomas Knoell* Shoes: *Martinez Valero* Hair: *Ramona Azcona* Makeup: *Monica Boyd-Lester*

RHONDA
Pages 9, 47, 93, 101, 138, 161
Dress: *San Patrick* Jewelry: *her own* Shoes: *Jessica Simpson* Hair: *Celinet Mendez* Makeup: *Monica Boyd-Lester* Flowers: *Stellar Style Events*

SHANNON
Pages 28, 33, 47, 77
Dress: *Pnina Tornai* Veil: *Occansey Designs* Jewelry: *Swarovski* Shoes: *RSVP* Hair: *Ramona Azcona* Makeup: *Christina Amador* Flowers: *Florisity*

SHOSHANNA
Page 162
Dress: *Judd Waddell* Shrug: *Kleinfeld Bridal* Veil: *Pinpoint Bridal* Jewelry: *her own* Shoes: *Calvin Klein* Hair: *Ramona Azcona* Makeup: *Christina Amador* Flowers: *Stellar Style Events*

SUSAN
Pages 83, 143, 172
Dress: *Pnina Tornai* Jewelry: *her own* Headpiece: *Victoria Bridal* Shoes: *Dyeables* Hair: *Celinet Mendez* Makeup: *Ramona Azcona* Flowers: *Florisity*

TINA
Page 118
Dress: *Elizabeth Fillmore (courtesy Kleinfeld Bridal)* Hair: *Jeanne Carosone* Makeup: *Christina Amador* Tattoo Embellishments: *Lisa Juarez-Russo* Flowers: *Florisity*

....

Pages 64-65 Fabrics provided by *Super Textiles*. Page 69 Laces provided by *Gelmor Lace*. Page 127 Mood Board by Eric Hoffman Photos

by Jonathan Rubin. *Page 186* Tuxedo, Shirt, Vest, Pocket Square provided by *Kleinfeld Men;* Bow tie *by Gucci* from Randy's private collection; Boutonniere provided by *Florisity*. *Page 199 Tiffany* Watch, *Gucci* Shoes and Tie from Randy's private collection; Cufflinks, Rings, Atomizer, Shoe Horn from Eric's private collection; Pocket Square provided by *Kleinfeld Men;* Boutonniere provided by *Florisity*.

....

RANDY FENOLI
Throughout
Suit: *Randy Fenoli for Kleinfeld Men* Shirt: *Custom made by CEGO, NYC* Tie: *Duchamp* Pocket Square: *From Randy's personal collection* Cufflinks: *Custom made by Randy Fenoli* Socks: *Paul Smith* Shoes: *Gucci Made to Order* Ring: *Tiffany & Co* Watch: *Gucci* Hair: *Randy Fenoli*

ABOUT THE AUTHOR

As the star of TLC's *Say Yes to the Dress*, *Say Yes to the Dress: Big Bliss*, and *Randy Knows Best*, Randy Fenoli, Fashion Director at the famous Kleinfeld bridal salon, is seen by millions of viewers and works with nearly 15,000 brides a year.

Randy has a degree from the Fashion Institute of Technology, where he won a number of awards for bridal design and achievement. Immediately after graduating, he launched two bridal industry collections: Randy Fenoli for the Diamond Collection and Randy Fenoli for Dessy Creations. Randy is the recipient of two Design Excellence in the Bridal Industry (DEBI) awards, the most prestigious award for bridal designers.

Besides being featured on the *Say Yes to the Dress* shows, Randy was a correspondent for TLC's coverage of the royal wedding of Prince William and Kate Middleton and has worked as a fashion commentator for the Associated Press on the red carpet of the 2010 Academy Awards.

Randy lives in New York City with partner, Michael, and beloved dogs Maggie and Bandit.

INDEX